THE SECRET WAY

Volume I

RITUAL ABUSE IN ECKANKAR

J.N. SYKES

Freedom from Cult Abuse Inc.

THE SECRET WAY: RITUAL ABUSE IN ECKANKAR

The Secret Way Volume I: Ritual Abuse in Eckankar

1st edition

Typeset in Georgia

ISBN: 9798714800122 (paperback)

Imprint: Independently published in Kindle, e-book and paperback.

THE SECRET WAY

Volume I

RITUAL ABUSE IN ECKANKAR

INTRODUCTION

The Secret Way series is a deep dive into the inner self of the Eckankar cult, into its secret practices, occult rituals, and terrifying use of compelling thought control to discipline initiates and demoralise leavers.

The first volume in this series, *The Secret Way: Ritual Abuse in Eckankar*, provides a clear introduction to this complex subject and a detailed history of ritual abuse directed at a leaver, the author.

The author himself is a former member of 14 years, so this is an insider's view. The author shares insights and knowledge learned in over 40 years of religious and spiritual experience, including in his adopted Christian faith, which expose this damaging cult to a new, harsh light.

To Eckankar initiates who dismiss all this as irrelevant, as they can experience 'the light and sound of Eck', a word of warning. Those experiences have *nothing* to do with God or the Holy Spirit, and everything to do with a group of highly disciplined, violent and obsessive Tibetan monks who make Western black magicians look like a bunch of reckless, ill-advised schooldchildren.

Those experiences are nothing more than thought projections. The feeling of being in touch with God or 'the Sugmad' is a projection into your mind and onto your emotions. Such projections may appear compelling and credible. They are however entirely false.

The author knows this as a certainty for one reason. Unlike Mr Klemp, a failed Christian, and the initiates of Eckankar, the author has actually experienced the Holy Spirit directly. It is a world away from the sensory experiences offered in Eckankar. It is God's Being Itself.

This book is a wake-up call to those who think that membership means a nice, easy ride to God. It's actually a nice, easy ride into profound illusion.

March 2021

PART I

RITUAL ABUSE
AND TORTURE IN
ECKANKAR

THE SECRET WAY: RITUAL ABUSE IN ECKANKAR

1

RITUAL ABUSE IN ECKANKAR

Eckankar demands absolute obedience to Harold Klemp, the former psychiatric patient and criminal detainee who claims to be directly appointed by God as the world's spiritual leader.

If you obey him, Klemp appears to you in your mind and in your dreams, and spins fantastical 3D experiences like LSD trips.

If you disobey him, however, it's very different. Klemp still appears to you in your mind, and in your home as a semi-physical presence, but accompanied by demons, apparitions, shapeless creatures that grab your back, etc.

Klemp uses instant thought projection, which attacks the thought content of the target's mind. It is an old black magic technique in which Klemp is quite expert.

These terrifying experiences are outtakes from the Exorcist movie. They're presented with objective clarity, so you always know that you are being punished for being disobedient.
Ritual abuses to which Joe Sykes was subjected for 26 years include:

(1) sleep deprivation: waking him up every 45-60 minutes, cutting sleep off after 3 hours by presenting creatures that appear to attack or talking at him accusatorily;

(2) sleep disturbances: disrupting his dream periods with disturbing dreams negatively re-presenting people and situations in his life;

(3) digestive attack: causing inflamed intestines by projecting violent power at the abdomen, inserting sharp needles or belts of needles, locking draining tubes onto the stomach, all causative of watery diarrhoea, and physical weakness.

Not very 'spiritual' as it turns out.

Eckankar, a sham religion, talks fantastical talk to distract members from the oppressive nature of the group. It's a kind of Gestapo organisation disguised as a neighbourhood charity.

Which it is not.

The cult poses serious dangers to Minnesotan communities because it is territorial. Until it has to leave, as it had to leave California in the 1980s amidst scandals involving leaders' adultery with wives and theft of corporate funds of $2.5m, Eckankar beds itself down on land and claims it.

They move into the community and seek to 'enlighten' it by bringing in to people's lives a secret group of 571 dead 'Masters' based in Tibet.

Eckankar members pose as ordinary people, working jobs, raising families, attending schools. Meanwhile they have a secret life involving the invocation of and obedience to these dead Masters who they call 'the Eck Masters'.

These Masters are also territorial. They appear alongside Klemp to members and their families in their minds and in their dreams.

They establish and enforce their influence and control over members and their relatives, friends, acquaintances, and work colleagues.

This may sound a tad far-fetched but the cult sells pictures of these dead Masters holding midnight meetings in remote Tibet.

The cult claims one of these dead Masters is its former leader Paul Twitchell. Twitchell founded the cult in California in 1965 as a New Age Hindu cult based on guru worship of himself. Twitchell passed in 1971 but Eckankar asserts Twitchell still appears to members with over twenty Masters sporting names such as 'Rebazar Tarzs' and 'Yaubl Saccabi'.

Eckankar members sing 'Hu' in groups. In their minds and in initiations every few years they get visited by various kinds of spirits.

Some of these are extremely small, appearing as coloured lights, or making high-pitched sounds.

One is placed on top of the member's head. This demon is known to deliverance ministers as 'the demon of the top spot.' Secondly, members meet weekly in which they chant demonic sounds that cause the human leader (currently Harold Klemp, from Wisconsin) and the said earthbound spirits to manifest their presence.

This is what deliverance ministers call the invocation of demons

Thirdly, Eckankar initiates members every few years into one of 14 initiations in which members are introduced to and infested with new spirits. These members are living demon carriers.

A Catholic exorcist, or Protestant deliverance minister would put it simply. They would say Eckankar is invoking demonic spirits into Minnesotan communities, which latch onto individuals and claim their lives.

It is hard work to remove a batch of demonic spirits from each individual.

It's easier to grow a tree year by year than to cleanse a patch of fouled ground of overrunning weeds.

Deliverance ministers and exorcists would urge each of you to pray in the Holy Spirit around each church member and church, and into your communities, diligently on a daily basis, to protect yourselves from this psychically corrosive cult.

We take a different approach, though we applaud exorcists and deliverance ministers for their work and encourage churches to fund it specifically.

Harm done to Eckankar members

Our approach in Freedom From Cult Abuse ('FFCA') is to look at what kind of cult Eckankar actually is, and what it does to members and ex-members.

Eckankar is not a religion, nor is it a charity. Eckankar does not help people find God. It controls their minds using sophisticated thought control systems, and demand absolute obedience to Klemp and to the cult.

Members are deluded into believing they make spiritual progress, while they are merely psychologically entrapped.

Harms done to members as a result include loss of independence, lack of normal personal growth, gradual loss of natural social skills (so they have to fake their social interactions).

Members pay annual subscriptions and extra monies for seminars and other fundraising activities, believing they are helping the cause. In fact their paying for the leaders' homes, cars, salaries and corporate jets. It is a familiar but pathetic spectacle.

In the result, Eckankar is a terror organisation quite as harmful to a member's mind and emotional personality as ISIS was in Syria. It promises personal progress while using mind to mind control techniques to deny personal growth.

The cult's background is that the Minneapolis-based 'Eckankar' cult began operations in San Francisco in 1965 as a New Age cult.

It mixed then-fashionable astral travel, Sant Mat Hindu mysticism, and a culture of strict obedience to the leader that reflected the founder's Catholic and Freemasonry influences as well as his crippling personal insecurity.

The secret core, however, was Tibetan dark magic, of a particularly enslaving and destructive type.

There were a number of signs of the Tibetan influence. The founder and successors worshipped a group of Tibetan monks, all black magicians, with fanciful names like Rebazar Tarzs and Yaubl Saccabi.

THE SECRET WAY: RITUAL ABUSE IN ECKANKAR

The new Eckankar Master was said to be appointed in Tibet at midnight on 22 October, in the (mythical) valley of Tirmir.

In 1981 a new leader, Harold Klemp, who had lapsed from his Lutheran church in Wisconsin, where he had trained to be a minister, took control of the cult at a time of controversy where the previous leader, Darwin Gross, was accused of stealing $2.5m and a number of senior initiates' wives.

In the conflict that raged 1981-1987 between the Klemp and Gross camps, both leaders accused the other of practising *'the dark arts.'*

Klemp repackaged the cult as a 'religious church' so as to avoid tax on monies extracted from members. Klemp introduced semi-Christian concepts of 'church', 'clergy', religious ceremonies, etc, to disguise the fact Eckankar is a guru worship cult with Klemp as guru, dedicated to absolute control over members and their incomes.

2

TECHNIQUES OF TORMENT

Harold John Klemp and his agents caused a continuing invasion of privacy of Mr J.N. Sykes, a Christian convert and former initiate of the Eckankar cult. The assaults intensified from April 2018 when Mr Sykes began preparing litigation about his 26 years of suffering direct violent attack on his mind, emotions and body from Klemp and his associates.

This attack was always presented objectively, with start and stop times, and thoughts coming into the target's mind afterwards, briefly explaining the reason for the attack. Usually some reason based on an alleged flaw in the target's character.

The Californian cult Eckankar, escaped to Minneapolis in the 1980s in a storm of sexual and financial scandal, used controlling telepathy and thought control to injure a former member planning tort claims against the cult and its 'living eck master' Harold John Klemp, according to prospective plaintiff Joe Sykes.

Eckankar claims the highest being is 'the Sugmad', and that the Sugmad appointed Klemp in 1981 as cult leader.

As a matter of record, Klemp was appointed by the cult's Board of Trustees in 1981. That followed the Board's dismissal of former leader Darwin Gross for theft of over $2m. It is unclear if the money was returned.

Eckankar further claims that the Sugmad issues a spirit called 'the eck.' This 'eck' is studied by cult members. It is, they say, the primal spiritual force. Members, who are called 'initiates' or 'high initiates', practice in part by chanting short Hindi and other Asian words like 'hu' to 'the eck'.

As a matter of record, the cult's theology and practice is copied wholesale, without acknowledgment, from the books of JP Johnson and Kirpal Singh. A copyright theft lawsuit against Eckankar is being considered.

Mr Klemp deployed the following methods against Mr Sykes:

(1) Threats of terminal illness and death, made by the Eckankar spiritual leader;

(2) Using concentrated telepathy to appear as a 3D image in front of Mr J.N.Sykes, Mr Klemp inserts 'needles' into Mr Sykes' stomach, and 'clamps' on his intestines, causing violent diarrhoea and forcing him to take medication;

(3) Putting a 'cloak' on Mr J.N.Sykes's shoulders then projecting intensely violent power onto it, like a thunder in a heavy storm;

(4) Appearing in Mr J.N.Sykes' home and directing unbearably intense power at the back of his head and his upper back until Mr J.N.Sykes wants to scream or run;

(5) Appearing in Mr J.N.Sykes's dreams and regarding him reproachfully, as if to say, 'Why would you want to do this?'

Mr Klemp's autobiography 'Child in the Wilderness' describes similarly unbearable pressure being applied to him while an Eckankar member.

In fairness and in the interest of balanced reporting, it is noted the treatment inflicted on the current Eckankar leader as described by him in detail is not official Eckankar theology or practice. Eckankar denies subjecting any 'initiate' to torture.

The Eckankar leader in 'Child' tells candidly how that same application of unbearable pressure to his body and mind caused him to:

(1) feel he was commanded to take his clothes off in public in the Milwaukee airport lounge;

(2) be detained in a psychiatric institution in Wisconsin;

(3) jump off a bridge in Wisconsin in mid-winter to commit suicide.

The apparent point of this confession is first to indicate the cult requires absolute obedience in the case of certain members, and for that to be demonstrated.

Second, by implication, to warn disobedient members (or ex-members) of the punitive methods that can be applied to them.

Mr Klemp told a conference the true story of a female ex-member who became a Lutheran, as Mr Klemp had once been.

He told how she was accused of being fat and vain in her dreams, how her marriage broke up, how she lost her job, all soon after she left the cult. She cracked under the pressure of these varied assaults and disasters, and returned to the cult.

It is therefore clear on Mr Klemp's own account how, while Eckankar will deny such practices, certain disobedient or resistant members or ex-members may be subjected to mental or emotional torture in order to bring them in line.

None of this arises from official Eckankar 'church' theology or practice.

Mr Sykes considers he survived these repeated assaults on his mind and emotions (with physical consequences) only because of the Christian faith he adopted after leaving Eckankar in 1993.

He considers the assaults continued because Mr Klemp objected then and now to Mr Sykes' refusal to accept him as spiritual leader.

Mr Sykes, who joined in 1981, recalls the then leader Darwin Gross never caused him any harm. Mr Gross was a powerful, effective leader. What were called 'psychic attacks' occurred outside the cult, not inside it.

According to Mr Sykes, all that changed with Mr Klemp's arrival in 1982. A compromise candidate for leader when Mr Gross was fired on unproven allegations of theft, Mr Klemp had a different style. He was remote, pretending to be friendly and warm while being suspicious of city people.

Mr Klemp, according to Mr Sykes, was an extremely insecure man, suspecting people didn't like him, particularly city people. Mr Sykes incurred his anger when he wrote Klemp a letter in 1991 offering to adapt a cult book as a screenplay.

Mr Sykes believes Mr Klemp felt he did not show him the respect his lofty position deserved. Whatever the reason, almost immediately after a rejection letter was sent, Mr Sykes experienced overwhelming and terrifying telepathic and though control attacks. These caused terrifying hallucinations, promoting suicidal thought.

Mr Sykes wrote about some of these attacks in his book 'Cult', which was published online.

They included horrific sensations of being attacked by flying creatures in his bedroom. At his local gym, Mr Sykes saw his regular changing room apparently filled with clouds of dirty filthy air, jets of violent air propelled across changing areas, and an unpleasant feeling of being crowded by people he could not see.

The most violent attacks of this kind occurred in the gym. Mr Sykes will give evidence he quit the gym to avoid the attacks. Consequently he put on weight.

Twenty years later Mr Sykes was invited to join a different gym. This time when Klemp projected his horrors at him, Mr Sykes saw them for what they were: medieval terrors designed to break him.

Mr Sykes experienced Klemp appear, as if he was a ghost, and throw several entities at him who jumped on him, as an intimidation method. Mr Sykes ignored the strange hallucinations and methodically showered and dressed.

Since deciding to bring litigation against Mr Klemp, Mr Sykes received murder threats from Mr Klemp threatening his death if he proceeded with the court case.

Mr Klemp perpetrated the following terrifying attacks using telepathic and thought control methods:

(1) Repeated sensations of insertion of 4 - 6 inch needles in his stomach, causing actual physical symptoms including local pain and violent diarrhoea;

(2) Visual sensations of clamps placed around large parts of his intestines, again causing violent diarrhoea;

(3) threats to cause Mr Sykes harm, voiced audibly in an American voice, including:

'I will make you an old man;

'You will not make it;

'You will never walk into a court room.'

Eckankar is a fake religion

The Minnesotan cult Eckankar is built on and is made of a series of deceptions. Let's list them:

1. Its claim to be the path of spiritual adventure, giving experience in soul travel, led by experienced soul travel, fails in reality as these so-called spiritual adventurers are not spiritualised at all.

2. They don't operate in a higher realm in their conduct. Their conduct from the boss downwards is horrific: bullying, terrorising, abusive, cold and vicious and cruel to initiates perceived as disobedient.

3. Eckankar claims it leads members to spiritual purity. Untrue. It holds members in a spell. Year by year, it sucks them

further in to a black hole of non-change. Time stands still. No one changes. The vital force of life is missing. Eckankar is a train stuck on a siding. Its inactivity and lack of personal growth is masked and glossed by brief sensory experiences tossed them by disturbed leaders.

4. The initiates excuse the errors of their leaders explicitly or at times implicitly because their leaders are 'spiritual' leaders. Sorry, that's unreal. There is no excuse for abuse.

5. Eckankar claims its leaders are spiritual masters. For real? Twitchell and Klemp were arrested and hospitalised in psychiatric facilities. Twitchell, Gross and Klemp were/are all adulterous and adulterers. There is no moral or spiritual standard to be found in them. They're human and flawed. They're not above anything; they're leaders but not spiritual leaders.

6. The group's wholesale plagiarism and copyright of other groups' theology and practice, are forgiven as their founder Twitchell was a rascal. Sorry, that's B.S. Theft is theft. Eckankar owes a lot of money to the copyright holders.

These knots of fake thought, here unravelled, run right through this group's thought life. Eckankar is a top to bottom deception.

Once the group stops believing its self-sold fakery, it may also be a Waco, Texas in the making.

Tax fraud by Eckankar

One of the issues we have against Eckankar, the failed cult, is its use of nonprofit corporation status in California and

Minnesota to avoid tax from or about 1975, a period of 43 years.

The organisation's nonprofit applications rest on its constitution by charitable trust deed as a a religion. It has a god, worship, church, priests, prayer. If it looks like a religion, it purports, it must be one.

This simplistic description does not address the widespread use of non religious methods of instilling fear in initiates: emotional duress, economic duress fior EIO staff, bullying in various forms by 5th and higher initiates, for the organisation to get what it wants.

Worse this description does not admit if the destructive telepathic and mind control techniques used by Twitchell on Klemp, Klemp on Darwin, Klemp on initiates.

Finally and worst of all it does not cover these destructive telepathic attacks on former initiates like Mr J.N.Sykes, Me Sykes.

Klemp and Eckankar have created a lot of victims over the 43 years.

That has nothing to do with religion. The concept of religion cannot be used as a cloak for torment and abuse of human beings.

It is criminally actionable conduct. It is also fraud on the states of California and Minnesita, and most particularly the IRS fir nondisclisure of material facts namely the applicant's implication and involvement in criminal conduct wholly inconsistent with religion.

Psychiatric records of Harold John Klemp

Klemp's psych records will make interesting reading when obtained and published.

The psych records concern his detention, following arrest by the Police, in a jail and then psychiatric facility in Wisconsin for bizarre conduct indicating severe mental health issues.

Klemp's psychiatric conduct included:

(1) fully undressing in Milwaukee international airport, in a public lounge;

(2) attempted suicide by jumping off a bridge in Wisconsin, in winter.

Klemp's criminal conduct was admitted in print in his autobiographical books, *Child in the Wilderness/A Modern Prophet*.

The pressure he describes he was under, which compelled him to behave criminally, is similar to the severe, serial pressure he and fellow Eckankar initiates under his control visited on Mr Sykes over a prolonged period.

As in Klemp's books, each of the attacks on Mr Sykes were presented objectively, employing severe duress and accompanying it with a clearly presented choice: obey, or be destroyed.

While Mr Klemp felt forced to act as he did, presumably by the leader and senior initiates of the time, Mr Sykes resisted the command to obey. That resulted in further and repeated assaults on Mr J.N.Sykes's mind and emotional well-being.

One question that arises from his admitted psychiatric conduct is his fitness to lead Eckankar, the Minnesotan cult, as its self-proclaimed 'spiritual leader.'

Another question that arises is whether he has deceived the Eckankar Board as to his mental fitness, on appointment in 1981. And continuing into the present.

A third question is whether he has deceived the cult membership as to his real medical state. He has presented himself to them as the highest servant of God, who he calls 'the Sugmad'. Whereas the truth may simply be he was mentally ill.

A fourth question is whether he so deceived Mr Sykes, in the course of his duties as the appointee of the Eckankar Board, titled 'the living eck master', during Mr Sykes' membership, and what consequences for Mr Sykes's own mental and emotional states he and the cult are liable for in law.

What the courts think of Eckankar

The courts have a low opinion of the Eckankar cult. Its moment has passed. Society has moved on. It is widely seen as yet another crazy religious cult. As an organisation prepared paranoiacally to bully, terrify, trespass on, and attack the body mind and emotions of those the leadership perceives as non-compliant.

Recently a court denied custody of her child to an initiate who played a tape of initiates singing 'hu'. The court deemed her unreliable as a result.

Understandable, right? The woman was in a cult.

Klemp's use of sleep destruction

Klemp won't let some leavers go. Those that don't matter he lets go (though many remain attached, merely disagreeing with the outward form of the cult). Where he has invested time and trouble, his attitude is, they're mine.

He's told stories of breaking leavers till they return. You will remember his story of the female leaver who became a Lutheran (published later in '*How to Find God*' by Klemp).

She was taunted in her dreams by Klemp and his gang, accusing her of being 'fat' and 'vain'.

She lost her job, then her marriage. Broken by the loneliness and poverty he'd caused her, she reapplied to the cult. She rejoined, minus her initiations.

The point of this story was that, if he wants, Klemp can break a leaver. A key element was his use of the dream state to attack. None of that is part of the official Eckankar religion that gets tax breaks. But it's what Klemp does.

Klemp has repeatedly used sleep deprivation on Mr J.N. Sykes. His diary records that for the last eight weeks, for example, Klemp has permitted him no more then 3 hours per night. After 3 hours, Mr Sykes is hit by power attacks precluding sleep.

The purpose of sleep destruction is always the same, whether used by the Soviets in psychiatric facilities on dissidents or by the British Army on the IRA: break the man's will.

Unfortunately for Mr Klemp, Mr Sykes is not going to break like the Lutheran leaver.

Mr Klemp is not going to be able to avoid trial of his appalling conduct.

Truly, Klemp should learn the merits of forgiveness. Whether he's a malicious black witch is beside the point. Forgiveness brings relief. It unlocks the cuffs of karma.

But for Klemp, who cannot forgive, who will not let go, there will be no relief.

3

IN THE ECKANKAR DUNGEON

Some believe the Eckankar cult founder Twitchell is the reincarnation of King Saul of Israel, later Saul of Tarsus, who took the name Paul.

Maybe, but look at the similarities. King Saul was famously insane and liable to drop into raving rage in a split second. Saul of Tarsus was the same. Both were aggressively and violently gay, with an obsession for young male flesh.

The point is that Saul of Tarsus persecuted Jesus' dedicated disciples. He imprisoned a number of them in a dungeon in Jerusalem. There Saul held them in large wooden machines which he used to extract information about the disciples, names and locations. The machines broke their bones.

Twitchell, similarly, delighted in torturing members out of sight of the crowd. Sometimes just through their mind. Darwin Gross was one such victim.

The author was another victim of Klemp's malicious, psychotic torture techniques. Klemp used the methods described in this book to torment the author until he complied. Klemp tried to put him in the Eckankar dungeon. Klemp failed, but persisted.

He caused pain and distress to the author and many of those around him, including family, friends, colleagues.

This book and its successors are a true record of ritual abuse in Eckankar directed at selected initiates and leavers.

PART TWO

RITUAL ABUSE AND
TORTURE
OF J.N.SYKES

4

BACKGROUND: ECKANKAR'S USE OF TORTURE AGAINST MR SYKES

From September 1992, Klemp and the Eckankar leadership began a programme of psychological torture against Mr Sykes to persuade him to obey them. The purpose was to break down his will and turn him into a cult servant. They were careful to rely on techniques difficult to trace back to them.

These are well known to practitioners of the occult and dark magic. They consist of thought control of the target, whereby the practitioner can project an image of himself instantly to the target and proceed to project focused, harmful thoughts into the target's mind and emotions, to create entities that behave like vicious demons but are in fact robotic thought creations.

The Eckankar techniques also include body-based torments similar to 'voodoo' except that instead of pins into dolls, Klemp and his colleagues use focused thought entities. For example, while a pin into a doll in the practitioner's office or home, that is based on the target, will create pain, illness, mental disorientation etc in the target, the Eckankar system uses the thought equivalent of the pin/doll combination; it creates perfectly focused thought entities like a knife, sword, demonic creature, etc, and projects them directly into the target's body.

While they are not physical, such thought forms can certainly destroy the physical body. However, being thought forms, they can equally be destroyed once identified.

For this reason Klemp usually introduces them in the sleep state, so the target wakes up in bodily torment, and is immediately disorientated or unsure how this state of pain was created.

Facts

The facts are, briefly, that Mr Sykes was a member of the cult from or about January 1980 to April 1993. While a member he studied the group's theological books, practiced the group's 'spiritual exercises' which involved worship of Mr Klemp, attended its seminars in the USA once or twice per year and in Europe, organized advertised and gave talks with a team explaining the group's theology and practice, gave talks in UK seminars, edited its UK newsletter for several years, performed music at its European and UK seminars, and in the result was an active participant in the group's activities.

In the late 1980s the cult's general counsel Douglas Kunin told Mr Sykes at a European seminar, 'You're our man in London.' In or about 1990-1991 Mr Sykes sent Mr Klemp a proposal to adapt a Cult book ('Talons of Time') into a screenplay. He and Mr. Kunin corresponded in that regard.

During this latter period Mr Sykes received information in his mind by hearing words or sensing a situation projected at him by Mr Klemp, that is, by telepathic communication. In September 1992 Mr Sykes complied with Mr Klemp's first direct telepathic instruction. He took an apartment in Ealing, an area of West London, UK.

From his first night in the Ealing apartment, Mr Sykes found himself under direct, violent telepathic attack from Mr Klemp. During the period September 1992 – early April 1993 Mr Sykes was unable to sleep properly, had stomach pains when he tried to eat, was unable to take employment or perform any useful function. Mr Sykes resigned in April 1993 and moved to a secret location.

In March 1994 Mr Sykes became a Christian. From Mr Sykes's resignation, however, Mr Klemp did not cease his attempts to use and to renew his telepathic influence over Mr Sykes's mind, as developed and refined during 14 years of membership. Mr Klemp's object appeared always to cause Mr Sykes to obey Mr Klemp, and in particular to cease to practice Christianity and to return to the cult group. Following litigation in the late 1990s, Mr Sykes focused on his Christian practice and on his legal practice.

As to whether the cult caused Mr Klemp to so act towards Mr Sykes, the cult was at all material times employed Mr Klemp as its purported spiritual leader with the title 'living eck master' and remunerated by regular payments of salary and pecuniary benefits including inter alia housing, cars, pension, and protection officers, and pursuant to that employment relationship (howsoever formulated and agreed) directed or agreed Mr Klemp's use of thought control techniques (also describable as brainwashing and mind control) against leavers and former members of the cult group including Mr Sykes, that intended to cause, or were reckless or negligent as to causing, tortious harm to them.

The use of thought control techniques to communicate with, and to assault, the mind and emotions of selected leavers like Mr Sykes was nonconsensual.

To understand this better, and how outrageous and destructive these techniques as practiced in Eckankar are, read Mr Klemp books published by the cult, including Mr Klemp's autobiography Child in the Wilderness, republished with new material as A Modern Prophet, and transcripts of his public talks.

This form of assault on the individual member and leaver is of course wholly inconsistent with the cult's official religious theology and practice. That promotes consensual communication between Mr Klemp and Cult members. This is characterised as 'soul travel,' although reasonably interpretable for evidential purposes (without imposing any semantic restriction nor imposing on Klemp and Eckankar' free use of the term 'soul travel') as communication by thought control or telepathy.

It is routinely described by members in the annual publication 'The Eckankar Journal' and the book 'In the Company of Eck Masters' by Phil Morimitsu. In those descriptions, Mr Klemp may appear to the member in their home, in public places, or in non-physical environments by projection of his physical appearance, in which he communicates with the member mentally and/or emotionally by conversation and/or involvement in sensory experience.

Mr. Morimitsu describes Mr Klemp appearing bodily to him out of thin air in his apartment (at pages 251 - 262). Mr Klemp is there named using his 'spiritual name', 'Wah Z.' Mr Klemp directs the member to visit a local library. While there, Mr Klemp points out they are now in ancient Atlantis. Mr.

Morimitsu notes the change in his surroundings. They take a ride in a space car through the ancient city and meet an ancient sage. Mr Klemp's control over Mr. Morimitsu's experience, or the contents of his mental perceptions, is complete.

However, the official Eckankar position is mere advertising. It is false and disingenuous. They don't mean what they say at all. They are just selling a story to acquire dollars. And they always need a lot of dollars, don't they?

The reality is Harold John Klemp and his colleagues directed thought control assaults on Mr Sykes at night from September 1992, to torment him, to render him unable to sleep, and during the day subjected him to violent assaults particularly when he was alone.

These assaults were at all times most intensive each week in the three days before Mr Sykes intended to attend a Christian church on a Sunday, preventing Mr Sykes from sleeping on Friday and Saturday nights.

The assaults were frequently coupled with verbal entreaties and commands to return to cult membership, from whose cult-like organization Mr Sykes resigned in April 1993 after a 14 year membership, or simply to obey Mr Klemp.

As a result Mr Sykes suffered severe emotional distress over a prolonged period.

5

WRITTEN ADMISSIONS OF RITUAL ABUSE BY KLEMP

Klemp and Eckankar have made a number of written admissions of conduct similar to that alleged by Mr Sykes. The admissions have been as noted above inconsistent and contradictory to their official theology and practice.

Their written admissions make overwhelmingly likely Mr Sykes's own claims.

Mr Klemp made written admissions of feeling compelled to do unlawful, sociopathic and/or psychopathic acts against his will in his autobiographical books 'Child in the Wilderness' published in 1989 by the cult's imprint Illuminated Way Press, and 'Autobiography of a Modern Prophet' published in 1996 by the cult, which contains similar as well as different incidents.

Mr Klemp gives as background and context to these acts his relationship with Paul Twitchell the then Cult leader. He describes incidents illustrating his obedient, close relationship with Mr. Twitchell. He describes Mr. Twitchell as his 'master' or guru, 'my spiritual mentor' (Child in the Wilderness, page 110). He details meetings with Mr. Twitchell in otherworldly settings and in dreams. It is strongly implied that the compulsive acts committed by him against his will in the central chapters derive from that relationship.

Mr. Klemp describes in Child in the Wilderness how he felt compelled to commit suicide. He did so by jumping off a bridge in a Wisconsin city in the middle of the night, in freezing midwinter (Child in the Wilderness, pp 127 – 128, 135 – 139, 141 - 147).

Mr. Klemp says at the climactic point: 'It was suddenly plain what had to be done next. I had to face my fear of death by jumping in the river' (p142).

The sequence was as follows. Earlier, he had been told by a bartender that that night he would face a challenge in which he had to comply with any command, no matter what. Secondly, before the night was out he would be riding in an ambulance. Thirdly, the bartender asked if Mr. Klemp was ready to face 'the Mountain of Yama' (pp 127 - 128). 'Yama' is Sanskrit for 'death'. In other words, the speaker in the story was advising Mr. Klemp he would have to face death.

Following that, Mr. Klemp meets a bridge-tender whose words cause him to wonder, in relation to being bold and adventuresome in seeking God, 'Might that include giving up one's life? I hoped not. The thought of death turned my blood cold' (p129). Next Mr. Klemp meets someone with the appearance of Mr. Twitchell, his guru, who is pointedly rude to him. The bridge-tender when leaving with this man asks Mr. Klemp: 'Remember the Mountain of Yama' (p138). Mr. Klemp translates this as 'the mountain of death' (p139). This is a reminder of the bartender's advice he would face the challenge of death that night.

Putting all these words together, Mr. Klemp realizes he has been challenged to face death or 'Yama' three times (p.142). He appears influenced by the fact the bridge-tender is in the company of a man resembling Mr. Twitchell the group founder and his guru.

As a result of all this, Mr. Klemp feels compelled to jump off the bridge (p142). 'It was plain what had to be done next.' In summary, this account is a description of Mr Klemp, leader of the cult group, being commanded to face death and commit suicide. It is inferable from the set of pages cited here that the command came into his mind from his mentor, Mr. Twitchell, and his associates.

Mr. Klemp was duly given medical care in hospital and taken home by the Police (Child in the Wilderness, pp. 153 – 157). Disclosure will be sought of the relevant criminal and/or psychiatric records from the Wisconsin authorities.

Mr. Klemp describes a different incident in the Departures lounge of Milwaukee Airport. There he suddenly felt compelled to remove all his clothes in front of members of the public in the packed lounge (Child in the Wilderness, pp 166 mid-page - 172).

He describes how he felt sick at heart at the prospect of undressing, and in undressing: 'Waiting for the next flight to board I pondered what else I might do to achieve complete surrender. Then the thought came to disrobe. Sick at heart, I nonetheless got up to follow out the latest instructions.' (p172). However, he felt compelled to obey the command in his mind to undress in public.

Immediately before the command to undress, he heard a voice telling him that Paul Twitchell was in the airport and wanted to see him. (Mr. Twitchell was then in Europe, see p166). It is inferable from the context the command came into his mind from Mr. Twitchell.

Mr. Klemp was duly arrested, detained (p173 - 174), jailed (pp178 – 183), and given a choice of facing charges of disturbing the peace or indefinite confinement in the county hospital for psychiatric evaluation (pp184 – 185). He relates: 'What this came down to was to commit myself to a hospital for an indefinite stay, to undergo psychological evaluation' (p184).

Mr. Klemp attended court where the Judge read out the assistant DA's offer of psychiatric examination in the county hospital and the prisoner agreed. He was duly sentenced to be held in the county hospital for examination (p189-190). (Query whether the arrest was for disturbing the peace or indecent exposure, as to which disclosure is sought).

The upshot was Mr. Klemp was (like Mr. Twitchell before him) detained in a psychiatric facility in Wisconsin for a period of time (p192 - 232). He claims it was 'three weeks' (p191, 206). Disclosure will be sought of the relevant criminal and/or psychiatric records from the Wisconsin authorities.

In a third incident in Child in the Wilderness, on a different point, Mr. Klemp describes how as an employee in a printing workshop, he directed a beam of psychic power into the workshop (in chapter 12, Bedlam in the Proofroom, pages 107 – 118, at pp 116 - 118). This beam of power adversely affected the printing staff and their environment. It is implied that Mr. Klemp had the ability to create, control and focus some kind of power, presumably through his mind. Further, that he could use that power to cause harm to others and to the environment of others.

These incidents are directly relevant to Mr Sykes's claims as set out below. They share essential common features. These include:

(1) the use of thought control by the group's leader against the member;

(2) the compulsive command which must be obeyed;

(3) the use of thought to communicate the command to the member;

(4) the infliction of emotional humiliation and degradation on the member;

(5) the ability to create, control and focus mental powers at others to cause harm.

If it is said that these incidents were religious experiences occurring within the cult's religious framework, they are wholly inconsistent with the official theology and practice of the cult which effectively claims to provide spiritual education of a non-harmful, consensual type.

There is no provision anywhere in its theology or practice for suicide, public indecency, commands to do unlawful sociopathic or psychopathic acts. There is no provision for the use of mental or other powers to harm other people and their environment. The incidents admitted by Mr Klemp simply do not fit within the cult's official stance.

In any event while there are common features supportive of Mr Sykes's claims against Klemp and Eckankar, there are features that differ. Those include:

(1) Mr Sykes was at all material times an ex-member of and third party to the cult;

(2) Mr Sykes was then a member of a different religion, Christianity;

(3) Mr. Klemp's actions towards Mr Sykes were hostile and non-consensual;

(4) the conduct complained of occurred outside and inconsistent with the cult's official theology and practice, ie it was outside the religious framework of the church;

(5) the conduct complained of was not only nonconsensual but caused Mr Sykes severe emotional distress, and thereby gave rise to civil liability.

Mr Klemp made admissions of mental assaults on members and/or leavers in writing. These admissions were, again, outwith and wholly inconsistent with the cult's theology and practice. They were published by the cult.

In one striking case, Mr Klemp gave an account in a public talk at a Cult seminar of the gradual breaking of the will of a leaver. The account was published in his book Unlocking the Puzzle Box, the Mahanta Transcripts Book 6, at pages 211 – 214, headed 'A lesson in vanity.' The publisher was the cult imprint the Illuminated Way Press.

Mr Klemp described how a female member became disillusioned with the group because of her lack of progress. She was criticized in a dream by four Cult 'spiritual masters' for being 'vain', in failing to surrender her will to them.

In another incident, two Cult 'spiritual masters' met her and criticized her for being overweight, querying, 'Why are you in a fat body?'

She resigned from the group, and became a Lutheran. She had a weight reduction operation, but subsequently lost her marriage. At the point she gave up on her husband, and was now alone, she re-experienced a 'golden light' she associated with the cult, left the Lutheran church, and returned to the group.

The cult, who appeared to have first-hand knowledge of these dramatic events, implied in his account that the strain of criticism while in the group, and the collapse of her marriage while a Lutheran, broke the leaver's will. At the point her will broke, she obediently returned to membership.

Separately, the cult published threatening statements directed at members in a number of books. These threats advised members their alternatives were to obey the Eckankar leader or to suffer eternal pain.

In Letters to a Chela, at page 107, Mr. Twitchell wrote: "Anyone who breaks away from Eck after receiving the initiation into Eck, will have to go through many future lives until he meets the Eck Master again and accepts him to be the Living Eck Master and surrenders to him completely."

In the group's 'bible', The Shariyat ki Sugmad II, at page 182, Twitchell explained the importance of following the group's leader: "The Mahanta, the Living Eck Master, is the only being who is eligible to make known the true path to God. All others mislead their followers, because they themselves are misled."

In a third book, the Spiritual Notebook, at page 196, Twitchell wrote this: 'Within the Shariyat-Ki-Sugmad is found the quotation: "He who leaves the path of ECK, or refuses to follow it, shall dwell in the astral hells until the Master takes mercy upon him and brings him upon the path again." ' The threat was that a leaver or disobedient member would suffer a long painful existence while confined to a 'hell.'

In The Shariyat-Ki-Sugmad II, at page 166, Twitchell threatened terrible consequences for a leaver: "Woe be unto him if he does (resign), for it is known among those who have reached these lofty heights and witnessed the consequences of the few who have. Those few have found that spiritual decay sets in immediately, affecting the health, material life and spiritual life, and brings death more swiftly."

This threat was an explicit threat that if a member resigned, their health and material existence would decay, leading to an early death.   It is typical of the cult.   They use threats of loss of spiritual progress, of death, to intimidate, both verbally and in their literature.

6

INCIDENTS OF RITUAL ABUSE

The following records begin in June 2017. Before then Mr Sykes did not keep detailed records. However, he was subjected to similar attacks from September 1992.

June – December 2017

On Sunday 18th June 2017 Mr Sykes was subjected by Mr Klemp (hereinafter Mr. Klemp) to telepathic and/or remote thought control attack when at or about 5 a.m. he appeared in Mr Sykes's bedroom and hit him repeatedly on the back to prevent him sleeping.

Mr Sykes emailed his church for prayer at 5.55 a.m. describing the incident.

By way of background, this was the latest incident in serial assaults on Mr Sykes in relation to his Christian church attendance. They began when, having resigned from Mr Klemp in April 1993, he became a regular attendee at Sunday Christian church services from or about March 1994. Mr.

Klemp assaulted Mr Sykes inferrably with the object of dissuading or preventing him attending a competitor church.

The assault was not physical, but effected by Mr Klemp`s residual telepathic influence over Mr Sykes deriving from his 14 year membership 1980 – 1993, and Mr. Klemp`s use of Mr Klemp's thought control techniques for harmful purposes.

As to the telepathic influence, this was established between Mr Sykes and Mr. Klemp in the period 1982 – 1984. Mr Klemp typically establishes a relationship of telepathic influence between member and leader in the first two years of membership. This is achieved by the member's practice of 'soul travel' exercises. These are a form of meditation in which the member chants a simple sound and focusses inwardly on his mind's eye. Mr Sykes's typical experience was the leader appeared to him in his mind's eye as a blue light or in his habitual form. The leader spoke to him or projected a thought-based sensory experience into his mind. Experiences of members seeing Mr. Klemp in their mind's eye and hearing him speak during soul travel exercises or in dreams are routinely described in detail inter alia in Mr Klemp's annual publication The Eckankar Journal. Effectively, Mr. Klemp took control of the member's mind and senses during at those times.

Mr Sykes's regular practice of 'soul travel' exercises had the effect of his voluntarily opening his mind to the influence of the leader. From October 1981 the group leader was Mr. Klemp. Over the period of Mr Sykes's membership, a considerable degree of influence was established by Mr. Klemp over Mr Sykes's mind and senses.

As to Mr. Klemp's use of thought control techniques, while Mr Sykes was a member these consisted of consensual projection of thought into Mr Sykes's mind. That was permissible within the confines of membership, and no criticism is made of it.

When Mr Sykes left the group in April 1993, however, Mr. Klemp used his thought control expertise and his influence over Mr Sykes's mind and senses to project non-consensual, threatening and oppressive words and alarming or terrifying sensory experiences into Mr Sykes's mind and senses. This was, therefore, the unlawful abuse of Mr Klemp's development of influence over Mr Sykes's mind and senses through long use of 'soul travel' exercises to harm him mentally and emotionally once he left, thereby inflicting on him severe emotional distress.

Mr Sykes considers the purpose of these assaults was the enforcement of group discipline. That is, to terrify him back into membership.

On 22nd June 2017 at 2.57am, Mr Sykes was assaulted by Mr Klemp and his associates in a London hotel room where he had taken refuge due to the assaults on him at home. He had been given a discounted luxury room, which was nice and clean. When Mr Sykes came out of the bathroom after getting ready for bed, however, he found demon-like entities hitting him as he walked towards the bed. Then he was hit in the head and suddenly found the entities were trying to stop him moving. He kept going and got between the sheets which were white and clean. Abruptly he was hit from above. He was unable to think. I tried to watch TV. Mr Sykes could not concentrate on the television. He felt the sheets becoming filthy under him. He looked at them and saw they were no longer clean but looked used and dirty.

On 2nd July 2017 Mr Sykes was followed into his home by Mr. Klemp, despite telling him he could not enter. Mr Sykes felt the peace of prayer from his church in the bedroom. He made and ate a snack in the kitchen with his pain relief medication. He returned to the bedroom and got on the bed. The pillows felt violent. Mr Sykes sensed there was some kind of invisible frame fixed over the pillows. One side of the bed was now wet.

He wished he had not come home. He thought, They are turning my lovely bedroom into a torture chamber. Then he heard Mr Klemp's voice say: 'Turn.'

On 19th July 2017 Mr Sykes emailed his church for prayer, asking them to remove the cult leader from the hotel bedroom so he could sleep. The email said the leader was stabbing him repeatedly in the stomach. Mr Sykes wrote, 'I have removed one occult knife after another in the spirit today. It is now midnight.'

On 3rd August 2017 at 5.42 am Mr Sykes emailed his church for prayer. Mr Sykes said he went to church the previous day. He came home exhausted. He felt he had been drained of energy the night before that (the 1st August), perhaps to make him feel too tired to attend. On the night of the 3rd August Mr Klemp projected his image at him when he went to bed. Following that, Mr Klemp hit the back of his head through the night, forced him to leave the bed by hitting his bladder during sleep waking him and causing him to go to bathroom, where he put entities/creatures on Mr Sykes's back. At the time of writing, he felt even more drained, stressed, and under attack.

Mr Sykes wrote in the same email: 'The cult has never accepted my leaving and the leader continues to appear to me and ask me to return.'

On 30th August 2017 Mr Sykes emailed his church for prayer asking them to 'remove the cult leader from the hotel bedroom.' The email stated that 'At 2.40 am he appeared and put a wet creature on the bed. It is disgusting but I have not been able to get it off the bed! Also I realised he has been hitting my mind in dreams leaving me tense and exhausted.'

On 14th September 2017 Mr. Klemp and undiscerned associates assaulted Mr Sykes all night. Several persons including Mr. Klemp appeared to be in the bedroom. The sheets felt soiled and violent. At 3.11 am Mr Sykes emailed his church for prayer. At that point he heard Mr. Klemp say he would attack 'till dawn.'

On 17th September 2017 Mr Sykes was assaulted by Mr. Klemp in his kitchen. Mr Sykes had brought home food to eat. He prepared it then sat down to eat. Mr. Klemp appeared and hit him hard in the stomach, on his back, on his chair. Mr Sykes became unable to eat, think or do anything. Mr Klemp started talking. He told Mr Sykes to take off his clothes. That was what happened to Mr Klemp while he was a member, as described in his book Child in the Wilderness.

On 24th September 2017 Mr Sykes emailed for prayer asking the church to remove 'the violent cult leader Mr Klemp' off him. Mr Sykes had brought back shopping and was putting it away in the kitchen. Mr Klemp abruptly appeared behind him, hitting his head with power, smashing power into the peace of the atmosphere around him. Mr Sykes started thinking of suicide just so it would stop. Then he went and washed his head and found Mr Klemp had attached there a kind of snake, approximately 9 inches wide and thick, and very long. Washing broke it off. Mr Klemp attached another in the same place. Mr Sykes went to email the church. Mr Klemp stopped immediately. He seems to fear Christians and Christian prayer.

On 30th September 2017 Mr Sykes emailed his church for prayer at night because Mr. Klemp was standing in his bedroom, at the end of the bed, fixing what appeared to be layers of filth over the sheets.

On 7th October 2017 Mr. Klemp returned to Mr Sykes's home, projecting his persona at him from Minnesota. Mr. Klemp hit Mr Sykes continuously from when he got home, and hit him with power in the bed, preventing sleep. At 5am he emailed the church for prayer. He noted that two days before, on 5th

October, Mr. Klemp had appeared to him and declared he (Mr Sykes) was the new Master of the cult.

On 8th October 2017 Mr Sykes went to bed at 12.18 am. At 1.15 am he emailed the church for prayer. Mr Sykes complained about Mr Klemp: 'He has hit me on the back, head and sheets continuously for an hour. The sheets that were dry and clean this morning - I finally slept properly for an hour after I think you prayed. They are now damp and infested with spirits.' The email continued: 'He is now making it crystal clear that if I come to my home I will not sleep and may commit suicide. His violent attack is so constant every day, appearing suddenly and attacking me in my office or on a bus, that at night I must sleep. That's when he hits hardest.' Mr Sykes concluded: 'I am so tired my brain aches for real sleep. The cult is once again using sleep deprivation to try to break me.'

On 23rd October 2017 Mr Sykes emailed for prayer to remove the cult leader from his bedroom: 'The cult leader is back with vengeance. He is the bedroom, cursing the sheets and me.' The email described what Mr Sykes had had to deal with: 'In the 2 hours I have been home, I had to remove demonic creatures from a chair in the kitchen so I could sit down. The chair was pretty nasty to sit in when I first tried. I have routinely removed his curses, foul projections and violent attacks on my back. It is all horror movie stuff, assigned by a disturbed mind.'

On 15th November 2017 Mr Sykes recorded another all night attack from Mr. Klemp: 'Harold Mr Klemp, the Eckankar cult leader, has turned up again and cursed doors, the bathroom, my head, back, the sheets on the bed - again. The sheets are so cursed I tried twice to lie on them and could not. They were being hit by too much power, like the glare of a mad demon.'

On 18th November 2017 Mr Sykes emailed for assistance: 'Please pray to remove the evil American from my bedroom and his curses in my body and the sheets. I am being tortured all night by Harold Mr Klemp, the American cult leader. I collapsed on the bed needing to rest. I got up and took my trousers off at 3.15am and went to the bathroom.'

Mr Sykes's account continued: 'I found the TV mysteriously turned on in the kitchen and turned it off. A picture of a whisky glass appeared to me. I heard Mr Klemp say, You will regret not taking that with you. I came back and as I got on the bed I was covered with a cloak of reptilian skin. I could not sleep. This horrible man directed power at the reptilian 'skin' continuously.'

Mr Sykes's account continued: 'Then he said, Take the shirt off. As it is freezing in the UK, I realised he wanted me to be cold, get a chill, and get sick. Maybe contract pneumonia and die. I tried to sleep again and finally gave up.'

On 7th December 2017 at 4.23 am Mr Sykes emailed his church for prayer, asking: Please may I have prayer to remove the violent man from the cult who is hitting me with power, creatures and hatred. I really need sleep.'

On 13th December 2017 at 3.04 am Mr Sykes emailed his church asking: 'May I please have prayer to remove the wet curses off the sheets and the violent cult member who is hitting me in the stomach right now (3.03am).' Later, Mr Sykes emailed the church updating them: 'The cult member is back after 2 hours. Please pray to remove him. He is in my bedroom pouring power onto my shirt, telling me to take it off (a favourite idea of his is clothes removal). It is impossible to sleep.'

<u>January – July 2018</u>

The following acts of subjection of Mr Sykes causing him severe emotional distress occurred in January – July 2018.

On 14th January 2018 Mr Sykes returned to his London home after a month away. He was due to spend one night before leaving for a trial. Arriving late, he went to bed at midnight. He was woken after one hour. He found he was covered with black demonic creatures. He felt the malicious presence of an Eckankar cult member. As Mr Sykes fought off the creatures, the cult member kept sending one after another at him. At 1.56am Mr Sykes emailed his church for prayer relief.

On 20th January 2018 Mr Sykes was attacked when he went to the bathroom in the middle of the night. He felt a jacket placed onto his back from behind. He ignored it. When he returned to the bedroom and approached the bed, he felt someone fit the jacket tightly onto his back. It felt like the inside of the dried skin of a demonic creature. Then he felt the skin was alive, and a creature behind it was devouring his back while hitting him repeatedly, inflicting pain. Mr Sykes tried to lie on his back. As he did so, he felt needles being stuck in the back of his neck. He heard people talking at him, under Mr Klemp's control. He realised the single object of all this activity was to prevent him gaining normal sleep.

On 23rd January 2018, the second night of Mr Sykes's trial in the city of Birmingham, he emailed for prayer relief. He recorded that on the first night he slept out of exhaustion. The only presence of Eckankar was a member appearing and saying in a sickly voice, 'You have been initiated into the highest order on the planet.' During the day, the first day of the trial, another Eckankar member appeared to him asking whether he was going to 'obey' them. At night, Mr Sykes felt followed by an

Eckankar member into the hotel room, where he sensed the member project a series of demonic creatures at him. Mr Sykes ignored the mental assault, rested, then did trial work for the next day. When he went to bed, it felt to him as if several Eckankar members were lying in the bed. He did not feel terrified, as doubtless was intended, but disgusted and furious.

Mr Sykes recognised these projected images of people, all male, as Eckankar members through his long membership; their attitude was distinctive, being confidently superior and hostile in a mode typical of Eckankar leaders who sense a member does not agree with them or Mr Klemp.

On Tuesday 30th January 2018 at 3.17am Mr Sykes emailed for prayer relief. He noted when he had returned home that night, after ten days away, it was quiet and peaceful. Within five minutes he felt Mr. Klemp appear and hit each room he entered with bursts of violent power. When he got on the bed, he felt Mr. Klemp place on his back what felt like an extremely violent cloak or coat. Next second, he felt power smashing into his back. He got off the bed, unable to endure the violence. He saw Mr. Klemp threw creatures and layers of filthy air onto the bed. He touched the sheets. Previously clean, they felt filthy to the touch. He heard Mr. Klemp say, 'I am satisfied.'

At 3.53 am Mr Sykes re-emailed for prayer relief. He recorded he was subject to an all-night attack, which felt prepared. He felt a group of Eckankar members hitting him on the back. He heard one of them demand he take off the t-shirt he was wearing. It was wintry and cold, and taking off a night garment would have risked a chill.

On 1st February 2018 during a typical night attack from Mr. Klemp, Mr Sykes heard a distinctive American voice say, 'You cannot live here any longer.'

On 4th February 2018 at 4.54am Mr Sykes emailed for prayer relief, specifically for Mr. Klemp (a violent cult member to be removed from his bedroom. The cult member had been hitting him repeatedly on his body, and stabbing him in his stomach. He had been doing so for several days, causing violent diarrhea.

Mr Sykes gave several examples in his email of what was occurring during the night attacks at that time:

1.   Standing behind him and hitting the back of his head.

2.,   Putting burning spells on his back.   Stabbing him repeatedly in the stomach until he has violent involuntary diarrhoea.

3.   Forcing intense pressure onto his bladder at least once during the day, causing him to urinate in his pants, on his legs.

Mr Sykes noted the contents of each attack were presented objectively to him, so that instead of simply being an attack it started and stopped leaving him perceiving it clearly and calmly. The result was he understood the cult's message was: rejoin the cult or suffer.

Mr Sykes noted this was precisely the message Mr Klemp boasted about in a public talk: Obey or be destroyed. Mr Sykes felt only that the attack was horrible and degrading to live through.

On 5th February 2018, at 1.33 am, Mr Sykes emailed for prayer relief during a violent attack from Mr. Klemp (who he then did not want to name). He asked for prayer 'to remove the violent cultist from off me/my stomach.' He recorded: 'I fell asleep on the bed after lying down for 5 minutes, out of sheer exhaustion. I woke 21/2 hours later and went to the bathroom. In 5 minutes, I was hit, prodded, finally back-cursed with another creature put on my back. It is 1.33am. I desperately need sleep. I have to be in court at 930. The cult member attacking me clearly wants to stop that.'

13.8 On 9th February 2018 at 4.16 am Mr Sykes recorded a particularly terrifying event in emailing for prayer. He recorded that he had fallen asleep out of exhaustion. The attack came at 3.30 am. Mr Klemp (named as 'the cultist' and 'the cultist who looks like the cult founder') hit him in the bedroom with several creatures. Some were three foot high. He could feel them angrily near him, some pushing themselves onto him. When he got on the bed, he felt his back hit by power. He realised Mr Klemp and his associated cult members were targeting his sleep. They obviously knew that without sleep, one could not cope with the day. In his case he had to get up at 6.30am, to go to the city of Reading on a 7.52 am train for a 10am court case. Mr Sykes felt Mr Klemp, appearing this time in the form of Paul Twitchell, the cult founder, knew full well how much he needed rest and was out to destroy it.

On Tuesday 14th February 2018 at 3.20 am, the night before a 1pm church service on 15th February 2018, Mr Sykes returned to the bedroom from the bathroom and felt a creature stuck on his upper back, gripping his right shoulder. He tried to get the creature off him. He succeeded, but it followed him onto the bed. He tried to ignore it, but he could not. He gave up trying to sleep again and went to the kitchen. He now realised the attack was intended to stop him attending church the next day. He noted in emailing for prayer that the cult had attacked his churchgoing every week since he became a Christian formally in 1994. Then he heard an American voice say: 'You don't want to go to church now, do you?'

On 23rd February 2018 Mr Sykes recorded another similar night attack from Klemp. 'Night' is a reference to UK time, usually six hours later than Minnesota time. Mr Sykes recorded he came back to the bedroom from the bathroom after two hours' sleep, after putting clean dry sheets on the bed. As he walked in the bedroom, he felt a creature was fixed on his back. He could not get it off. On the bed, he found the duvet cover was covered with heavy black creatures and cloak-like layers firmly clamped on it.

On 24th February 2018, at 1.06 am, Mr Sykes emailed for prayer relief, asking for prayer to remove 'the violent cultist and his attack creature he's using to stab me.'

The violent cultist was Harold John Klemp. The attack creature was a thought-created entity. Klemp routinely used thought-created entities to attack Mr Sykes. His entities can simulate human appearance or human features, human behaviour, but can also be shapeless or in the form of animals or demons. They can adopt weapons such as knives and can produce stabbing sensations. Such entities are a bit like computer programmes, following whatever instructions they are given.

Mr Sykes recorded that he 'collapsed exhausted on the bed then 'the head of the cult' (Mr Klemp) appeared and stabbed him in the centre of the stomach. Mr Klemp said (in a clear American voice): 'This is to stop you sleeping.' Mr Sykes worried that as he had eaten earlier, the simulated but sensorily real stabbing would turn hits meal to diarrhoea. He recalled Mr Klemp had used this trick 3 – 4 weeks ago, for a week.

On 25th February 2018, at 4.52 am, Saturday night going into Sunday morning, Mr Sykes sought prayer by email, asking for prayer to remove 'the psychotic cult leader' from his bedroom. Mr Sykes recorded the cult leader, ie Mr Klemp, had been hitting him for hours on the head, neck and back. Mr Sykes had been hearing Mr Klemp speaking to him quite clearly in his American accent, saying that he was not willing to let him sleep on clean sheets, and for Mr Sykes's own good he was going to 'curse' them. Mr Klemp had appeared to Mr Sykes on Saturday morning saying he would stop him sleeping that night. It appeared to Mr Sykes that Mr Klemp's actual aim was to prevent him sleeping, until he was too tired to attend church.

On 6th March 2018 at 6 am, in the bathroom, Mr Sykes felt a creature had stabbed him in the back, while a short man watched. Returning to the bedroom from the bathroom, another creature tried to stab Mr Sykes with a knife at the door. Mr Sykes went inside. The short man appeared there, then hit Mr Sykes with blasts of power. Mr Klemp appeared and threw what felt like snake-like creatures onto Mr Sykes's back. The sheets appeared covered with layers or 'cloaks' of filth.

On 8th March 2018 at 5.18pm Mr Sykes emailed for prayer relief, complaining that 'the violent cultist', Mr Klemp, was burning his back by attaching a cloak to his back that created a painful burning sensation, as if his skin was burning.

On 10th March 2018 Mr Klemp held an all-night attack on Mr Sykes, something he did no more than once every 3 months or so. Mr Sykes was tired from an emergency 10 hour meeting with a client. It was Saturday night, before Sunday morning church. Mr Sykes found the bedsheets became wet and filthy. He felt a violent demonic creature glare at him from behind his head.

On 13th March 2018 at 5.20 am Mr Sykes emailed for prayer asking for prayer to remove Mr Klemp, who he said had hit him repeatedly for the last three hours. Mr Sykes recorded that earlier he went home in a good mood, after gym and dinner. On the way home one of Klemp's people appeared to Mr Sykes and asked, 'Do you really want to go home?' By 5.20am, after three hours of attack, Mr Sykes's good mood was destroyed, and he was so traumatised he could not sleep. Mr Sykes noted that for the previous ten years he had spent much of the time staying at hotels, to avoid being attacked by Mr Klemp and his people in a place they knew. As Mr Sykes's business had gone down, he could no longer afford to spend most nights in a hotel. As a result, he was more at home, and Mr Klemp had increased the level of attack on his home.

On 14th March 2018 Mr Sykes found Mr Klemp hovering by the bed, near the pillows. He emailed his church stating he had removed seven layers of filth off the sheets, and various implements.

On 18th March 2018 Mr Klemp was in Mr Sykes's bedroom running another night attack, with the clean, dry bedsheets put on that morning now wet, feeling violent, and appearing to hold a mass of curses. The battle over the bedroom had continued through the morning. While Mr Sykes made the bed, he saw a group of Cult members projecting filth at the sheets. He went shopping. When he came back, he went into the bedroom. It now appeared like a dark hell. Later, after Mr Sykes had cleansed the sheets by breaking Klemp and Eckankar' projections off the room, a Cult member came quickly up behind Mr Sykes and placed a burning cloak on his back. Mr Sykes got into bed. The member got onto the bed, and hit Mr Sykes repeatedly from behind on the back, neck and head.

On about 1st May 2018 Mr Sykes emailed for prayer, stating Mr Klemp followed him to his home was terrorising him in the bedroom by, firstly, putting creatures on his back. Secondly, stabbing his stomach and intestines causing diarrhoea. Thirdly, waking him every 45 – 60 minutes precluding him from experiencing deep mental rest. Fourthly, attacking his mind # in the middle of the night for 2-3 hours so he was exhausted from lack of sleep

On 5th May 2018 Mr. Klemp woke Mr Sykes at 2am, after waking him every hour since going to bed. Each time he woke

Mr Sykes on the hour, Mr Sykes emerged from a violent dream. Mr. Klemp appeared in a ghostly form telling Mr Sykes he needs to stop his work in the lawsuit, and obey him instead. Finally, at 2am, Mr. Klemp kept him awake until 4am. In that period Mr. Klemp stood behind Mr Sykes hitting him in the back of the head with intense, stunning power, trying to induce a psychological breakdown. Then he stabbed Mr Sykes repeatedly in his stomach and abdomen, appearing to target his intestinal health. Mr Sykes called his church for prayer support. The attack faded away by 4 am.

Mr Sykes was reminded of techniques used against IRA prisoners by the British Army in Northern Ireland in the 1970s. The repeated waking from sleep, no deep sleep and no mental rest, the brutal infliction of attack on the body. Mr. Klemp cannot realistically hope to get away with all this. Mr Sykes considered Mr. Klemp was likely still psychiatrically damaged from his own early experiences in the cult leading to a Wisconsin court detaining him in a psychiatric hospital in the 1970s.

On 3rd July 2018, Mr Sykes discovered an hour after waking he was very short of physical and mental energy. It seemed to him 30% of his physical/nervous energies had been drained and stripped off his body and brain. Thoughts came into his mind that it was not worth it to sue the cult. Then Mr Sykes realized: Mr. Klemp was draining him of energy in an attempt to discourage me from litigating against him and his cult.

On 4th July 2018 Mr. Klemp appeared repeatedly in front of Mr Sykes, his face vicious. He appeared to insert tiny needles into Mr Sykes's stomach. A few hours later, Mr Sykes had to run to the bathroom, where he had violent diarrhoea. Mr Sykes reviewed these events. He recognised Mr. Klemp inserted needles or other tools into his stomach or intestines every time he had a protein-rich meal. Mr Sykes considered the purpose was to preclude him from receiving the nutritional benefit.

On 8th July 2018, Sunday morning, Mr. Klemp appeared looking a strange mixture of anxious and vicious. He appeared like a lost dog with sharp teeth, ready to snap and bite. There is no-one more vicious than a man who has fallen from the Christian faith towards someone who has found it.

On Wednesday 11th July 2018 Mr Sykes had planned to go to a different church. Which had a service at midday. The night before, Mr. Klemp appeared to hm and started all his usual tricks. From about 9pm he appeared to Mr Sykes, projecting sheer unrest and misery at him. Mr Sykes ignored him. At night when Mr Sykes got on the bed Mr. Klemp immediately hit him in the small of the back causing him pain. Mr Sykes then found there was a violent entity on the bed, which hit him, causing him additional discomfort. Finally, after sending a prayer request to his church, the attack faded and Mr Sykes finally slept. Two things always defeated Mr. Klemp and those who assisted him, causing them to leave: the presence of God and the presence of human love. Here it was the presence of God.

When Mr Sykes got ready for the day, and went to the bathroom, Mr. Klemp reappeared, stood behind him, and tried to attach several cloaks made of animal skin, which felt violent, and which were full of sharp needles. This time Mr Sykes stayed calm, deflecting the violent cloaks with clear, peaceful thought. Mr. Klemp refocused on the tap water coming out of the bathroom sink. As Mr Sykes washed, the water turned to filthy slime. It seemed to Mr Sykes this was straight out of the Exorcist.

The hatred from Mr. Klemp was so intense Mr Sykes remembered something his mother told him back in the 1990s: eat something first thing. Long after this, Mr Sykes analysed the pattern and realised Mr. Klemp really went for it when he sensed Mr Sykes's blood sugar was low. Mr Sykes left the bathroom, and ate something in the kitchen. The whole time Mr Sykes prepared the food, sat and ate it, Mr. Klemp stood behind him, talking like the rabid loon he really is. Mr Sykes ignored him and felt better for the food.

Back in the bedroom, as Mr Sykes got dressed, he felt Mr. Klemp's presence. Mr. Klemp attached violent creatures to his back. Then stood at the end of the bed, facing the bed, and poured a stream of filth onto the bed sheets. Mr Sykes was finally was so annoyed he decided to publish this incident online. Instantly Mr. Klemp pulled back.

Mr Sykes finished getting ready and turned to leave the bedroom. Mr. Klemp stood at the end of the bed and poured another stream of filth on the bed. Mr Sykes told him to get out, left, and checked the time. Dealing with all Mr. Klemp's attacks had made him late for church. Mr. Klemp had won. The fallen trainee priest had stopped Mr Sykes practising his chosen Christian faith by distracting him and so delaying him from attending church.

Mr Sykes then recalled that in the mid-2000s, when Mr. Klemp campaigned very hard to stop him attending his evangelical church each Sunday, Holy Trinity Brompton church in Knightsbridge, central London, near Harrods. Mr. Klemp had kept him awake all night Friday and Saturday every week for over three years, till he was too exhausted to attend. Mr. Klemp even attacked the sweet young married couple living in Earl's Court, London, who held the midweek evening Bible discussion and prayer group he attended, Mr Sykes felt each member of the circle received the invasive, destruction attentions of Mr. Klemp and perhaps other members who assisted him, during services and away from church. Everyone got tenser, looked a bit more tired.   They were extremely dedicated Christians who it would take a great deal to shake.

Then one night Mr. Klemp attacked the baby child of the young couple, who woke screaming in his pram during a prayer session. Mr Sykes went and looked. The baby was plainly disturbed. There was no obvious cause. He was clearly much loved, well wrapped, and before the meeting started had been entirely content. Mr Sykes knew right there Mr. Klemp had abused the baby. He decided never to return to the group, to avoid further attacks on the young couple resulting from his attendance. He telephoned the man's mother and resigned from the group. Soon after, in considerable distress, Mr Sykes left the church. The exhausting campaign to stop his attendance on Sunday, and the repeated attacks on these dedicated Christians, were too much for Mr Sykes. Recalling these events now, Mr Sykes realized Mr. Klemp was as viciously anti-Christian as ever.

On 12th July 2018 Mr Sykes returned home in a good mood. As he went inside, Mr. Klemp abruptly appeared and wrapped a creature around his shoulders. Mr. Klemp flared at Mr Sykes like a maniac. It took several minutes to break his intense attack off. Once inside, Mr Sykes reasoned Mr. Klemp was truly psychotic and irrational. Why bother with all these violent attacks? He had made Mr Sykes miserable but achieved nothing useful.

Later in the day, Mr Sykes remembered him appearing in the last few days and saying he would stop if he gave up the law case. Mr Sykes had laughed at that.

On Sunday 15th July 2018, the previous evening, after being terrified and exhausted by Mr. Klemp's attacks on Mr Sykes''s Christian practice, stopping him sleeping for 1-3 days before every church service, Mr Sykes decided he would not be bullied out of church attendance. Mr. Klemp had a different idea. Mr. Klemp woke him after just 3 ½ hours' sleep, at 530am. He summarily ordered Mr Sykes: 'Get up, you have had enough sleep.' Mr Sykes was tired out. He recognized from the pain at the back of his head (at the medulla oblongata) that Mr. Klemp had been hitting him continuously there while he half-slept, in a kind of superficial dreaming state. To break the power of the attack, Mr Sykes read a book until he fell asleep. He awoke at 10.30am. He would not make the morning service. Mr. Klemp had used the trick of waking him up after a disturbed sleep, breaking the sleep, so that he would not sleep to his normal time and get up in good time for church.

During breakfast Mr. Klemp stood watching Mr Sykes, who tried to ignore him. Mr Sykes distracted his mind by watching Columbo on TV. Mr Sykes washed up and went to the bathroom. Then he struck. The tap water became slimy under his hands. His towel was abruptly covered with layers of filth.

At this point, under the constant strain of Mr. Klemp's attacks, constant orders and suggestions that Mr Sykes abandon the planned lawsuit against him, combined with the effects of irregular and disturbed sleep, mind control attacks, and the daily disruption of his personal space, Mr Sykes wept. Mr. Klemp said: 'That's enough.' The attack fell off.

On 18th July 2018 Mr. Klemp was very angry with Mr Sykes. He said he wanted him to stop his lawsuit preparation and publishing these incidents online at the FFCA website. Mr Sykes rejected that. He determined he would not stop, because what Mr. Klemp has done to him is unlawful. As a legal practitioner Mr Sykes believes in the justice system. Trespass, assault, pressure to commit suicide, infliction of unbearable hatred and emotional pressures through telepathy is unlawful. The law recognises harassment can be communicated without physically spoken words or deeds. Mind control is already recognised in California and other states.

Later, Mr Sykes came home from the gym. Inside the block, he recognized there were living images of a cult member on each floor. As Mr Sykes went in his door, two of these living images or projections came around his front and back. He saw Mr. Klemp watching. He had created these images of men to frighten and intimidate me Mr Sykes.

On 20th July 2019, between 4pm and 8pm, when Mr Sykes was trying to catch up on sleep, Mr. Klemp, woke Mr Sykes four times, by pressurising his bladder. Each time he went to the bathroom, his bladder was not full. Mr Sykes prayed to restore calm, then got dressed. Brimming with violent anger, Mr. Klemp presented a series of entities to him, some short, some tall, each pressing violently on Mr Sykes^s stomach, some stabbing Mr Sykes, others standing on his feet so it felt they were coming into his clothes as he put them on.

These were alarming and disorientating assaults. For an outsider, at first this may seem hard to understand. But the weight of evidence is overwhelming. The overall picture is of Mr. Klemp departing from official Eckankar so-called religious doctrine and practice, and using powerful, specialised thought control and thought projection techniques to enforce his will on a refusenik like Mr Sykes. Eckankar literature assists Mr Sykes. Its doctrinal position is Mr. Klemp appears to members as 'the living eck master' using 'soul travel' to communicate with them. He appears in their home, or in other places, as a quasi-physical person. He is able to alter the appearance of their environment, and take them out of the body to other worlds.

What is not admitted in Eckankar doctrine or practice, is Mr. Klemp's use of thought control and thought projection to terrorise, trespass, assault on members or ex-members who will obey his supreme will. He is condemned out of his own mouth. His book Child in the Wilderness recounts how he himself was terrorised, his mind repeatedly assaulted. It is strongly implied this was done by the then leader of Eckankar, Paul Twitchell.

Mr. Klemp's own books admits to actors in the Eckankar cult using criminal assault against third parties. In the assaults recorded by Mr. Klemp in Child in the Wilderness, he is driven to such an extreme state of disorientation and distress, that he tried to commit suicide in midwinter in Wisconsin. This, from a former farm boy living on the open plains with descendants of German emigrants. Mr. Klemp's mind was so broken that he felt forced to take his own life. Mr. Klemp was also detained in a psychiatric hospital under court order after he took his clothes off in the departure lounge of Milwaukee airport.

It follows there is another Eckankar - one not admitted in the official Eckankar theology and practice - in which mental torture, powerful thought control and thought projection are used to batter the mind and emotions of a member until they are obedient to the leader.

Eckankar and Mr. Klemp however, went outside the confines of the membership of their group by deploying their destructive techniques at Mr Sykes on a daily basis since September 1992 in a manner accruing civil liability in the applicable limitation period.

On Saturday 21st July 2018 Mr. Klemp was in the room when the Claimant woke up. He ignored him. When he started dressing, he was suddenly pressured in the head by what felt like a hood, against which power was directed from three directions. Mr Sykes felt himself buckling under the sheer power of it. Then he felt Mr. Klemp's disturbed violent rage. He felt the hatred. Klemp had projected his personality to Mr Sykes's home to cause him pain out of sheer hatred. This appeared in part to because Mr Sykes, unlike Mr. Klemp, survived the violence in Eckankar and kept his independence and self-respect.

On 27th July 2018 Mr. Klemp projected his usual semi-ghostly form at Mr Sykes, for once relaxed and not asking Mr Sykes to give up his litigation. His new stance appeared to be he no longer cared. Whatever the result of the litigation, what he wanted was compliance from someone he selects for it.

On 29th July 2018, early Sunday morning, on cue Mr. Klemp appeared, as an insubstantial presence (but after 14 years in the cult Mr Sykes sensed him immediately). He asked, in a plain manner: 'Are you going to church?' Mr Sykes ignored him. It was a strange question given his full-on attack on Mr Sykes's churchgoing. Mr Sykes went to fix breakfast. He suddenly got an overwhelming urge to go to the bathroom. There he suffered sudden, violent diarrhoea. He knew his food intake was not the reason. It was the same diarrhoea he had had since March 2018. Mr Sykes felt his intestinal system had been pressured and subjected to intrusive, needle-like insertions. The result of the assault was that Mr. Klemp deprived Mr Sykes of vital body energies. It was inferable that was to weaken his litigation preparation.

8

FURTHER INCIDENTS OF RITUAL ABUSE

<u>August – December 2018</u>

The following incidents of severe emotional distress were inflicted on Mr Sykes in August – December 2018.

On 8th August 2018 Mr Klemp applied his new thought control technique of creating the sensation of placing 'knives' in his stomach and 'clamps' around his intestines. The result of the technique is mild inflammation of the intestines sufficient to cause semi-diarrhoea and 30% - 50% loss of nutritional value. This produces loss of vitality and discouragement. Spiritual techniques can thankfully combat these techniques. This day Mr Klemp WAS annoyed. He concentrated on Mr Sykes's intestines. He forced involuntary evacuation of his bowels. This was degrading and foul. Mr. Klemp said, 'That will teach you a lesson.'

On 15th August 2018 as Mr Sykes went to pack for travel overseas, having worked   late at the office to finish his casework. At home Mr Klemp using his telepathic and thought control techniques appeared to Mr Sykes without consent and attacked him maniacally on the head. Mr Klemp continued his attack so viciously and relentlessly that Mr Sykes was unable to concentrate on packing at all. He found the pitch and frequency of the violence unbearable. Mr Sykes sent an email from his phone requesting prayer from his church, setting out what happened.

Mr Sykes concluded Klemp and Eckankar had become much more violent, as they realised they are going to be sued by someone who knows and understands the

On the morning of 16th August 2018, following the previous night's attack by Mr Klemp, Mr Sykes suffered an attack of liquid diarrhoea. Mr. Klemp appeared to him, staring. It was clear he had again attacked my gut. I realised he had gone so far as to put what appeared to be thick, six inch high belts of some material, with violent entities armed with needles just outside the belt. I realised he was applying these techniques at night to inflame the stomach and intestines.

To that end Mr. Klemp said, in a very clear voice, 'A complete prohibition on food.' I realised he was going to try to use illness and loss of nutrition to break my spirit. These techniques risk injury and death to the target. I consider what he is doing to me as attempted murder.

On 31st August 2018 Mr Klemp appeared in Mr Sykes's holiday hotel at night. He woke Mr Sykes with bladder pressure. In the bathroom he fixed a creature onto Mr Sykes's lower spine. When Mr Sykes got back to the bed there was a man lying in it, sitting up. A creature the size of a 5 foot high winged demon was on the next bed, staring at Mr Sykes. These were terrifying things to see. Using his own power of thought, Mr Sykes broke the thoughts off him. Mr Klemp immediately restored them. Mr Sykes ended the attack by redirecting the manifestations onto Mr Klemp.

On Saturday 1st September 2018 Mr Sykes was praying in advance of church the next morning, Sunday morning. Mr Klemp appeared to him using the form of the group founder Paul Twitchell, as he sometimes does. He said, in the Twitchell persona: 'There is no point praying to Jesus. Harold performs the duties of Jesus as Jesus is dead. So praying to Jesus Christ is pointless as it is prayer to Harold!' Mr. Klemp was claiming to be Jesus, disrupting Mr Sykes's mental privacy in the process.

On 2nd September 1998, after church attendance, Mr Sykes woke during the night suffering sharp pains on the back of the head. He sensed a long creature with sharp needles inside the skin had been attached to the back of the head. He removed it. Mr Klemp appeared and said, 'This is severe.' Mr Sykes realised Mr Klemp had inflicted this 'penalty' on him for church attendance.

On 4th September 2018, when Mr Sykes went to the bathroom to perform an essential function, he felt Mr. Klemp abruptly appear behind him and attach a 'skin' to his back. Mr Sykes returned to the bed. He realized something was lying on the bed. He felt too tired to deal with it and craved sleep. Mr. Klemp hit him with a frenzied power until he was awake, and sleep was no longer possible.

On 11th September 2018 at 5am Mr. Klemp appeared in Mr Sykes's home. Mr Sykes had returned home the previous night from holidays. The apartment was peaceful. He woke at 5am with a burning desire to go to the bathroom. Mr. Klemp was waiting there. As Mr Sykes performed his function, Mr. Klemp placed a skin-like cloak on his back. Mr Sykes returned to the bedroom. He felt Mr. Klemp follow him. In the bedroom, Mr Sykes got on the bed. Mr. Klemp entered the room. He projected violent power onto the skin-like cloak, stopping Mr Sykes from returning to sleep. Mr. Klemp continued his attack for 3 ½ hours until 830am. By now Mr Sykes was crying from lack of sleep. Mr. Klemp said in a malicious tone: 'Call for prayer. I thought you would call for prayer.'

Mr. Klemp was referring to Mr Sykes asking Christian missionaries for prayer, to gain relief from Mr. Klemp's concentrated, obsessive attack on his mind and emotions.

Mr. Klemp's posture is that he is calm, modest, unconfident. It's a mask. The real person underneath is a nasty, revengeful man who never and forgets his early life as a farm boy, from which he ran. He despises and is envious anyone who has privileges he never had. from, poverty as a farm boy poverty. Considering the harm he has done me and others, claiming to be a modern guru, Mr. Klemp is alarmingly unspiritual. He is the most evil man I have met in 60 years on this Earth.

On 18th September 2018, after days of threats from Mr. Klemp appearing to Mr Sykes, stating he would never live to enter a courtroom, at night Mr Sykes returned home listening to Chick Corea jazz. As Mr Sykes entered his home, he felt Mr. Klemp appear behind him and slip inside the front door. As Mr Sykes closed the door, he felt his back and neck blasted with a violent power that stunned him. Mr Sykes told Mr. Klemp, or his presence, to leave. Mr. Klemp hit him repeatedly with violent power, bombing him with projections of hating violence that felt overwhelming. Mr Sykes ate something and calmed. He felt Mr. Klemp watching.

Then Mr. Klemp said, in a quiet voice:

'Had enough?'

On 2nd October 2018, at night, Mr Sykes was assaulted by Mr. Klemp after three hours of sleep. For the preceding eight weeks, Mr. Klemp had awoken Mr Sykes after three hours and made sure he could not go back to sleep. It was a classic method of breaking a prisoner used by the British in IRA prisons in the 1970s. Later, during the afternoon, Mr. Klemp returned when Mr Sykes was tired and weak from lack of sleep in his office. Mr. Klemp directed violent power at him.

On Sunday 14th October 2018, after Mr Sykes had attended church, Mr. Klemp appeared and said he would suffer for it. He added, with a half-grin, 'Tuesday's not Tuesday any more.'

Mr Klemp was referring back to his earlier routine of attack on my Christian practice. He had run the full routine every week rigorously from mid-1994 to or about the end of 2013. From 2014 he shortened the routine to the day before the church service. The night attacks typically disturbed Mr Sykes's attempts to sleep on Friday and Saturday nights with disorientating violent volleys of thought projection. That was routinely followed by a period of violent thought projection at Mr Sykes after the Sunday service, concluding Monday night or at the latest Tuesday morning. Relief usually came by Tuesday late morning.

Mr Klemp was now threatening to alter the routine. Mr Sykes sensed he meant the attack to come could overrun beyond Tuesday. Mr Sykes felt defenceless; Mr Klemp while sitting in a room in his home in the USA, understood to be in Minnesota, apparently sensed everything he did or planned to do

That night Mr. Klemp appeared in Mr Sykes's bedroom. He poured a shower of filthy air onto the clean sheets Mr Sykes put on the bed the previous night. Mr. Klemp then hit Mr Sykes's intestinal area and anus repeatedly, by projecting jets of power into those areas which caused sensory and then physical irritation. Mr. Klemp caused Mr Sykes's intestines and anus to contract and expand repeatedly until faeces started to be expelled. Mr Sykes found it disgusting and degrading. Mr. Klemp had the ability to concentrate on someone to the extent he broke through the barrier between thought and feeling and the physical body and its physical environment. Following the bathroom trip, Mr. Klemp woke Mr Sykes every hour. Mr. Klemp pressured Mr Sykes's bladder with intense concentrated thought such that he urinated while walking into the bathroom. Mr Sykes, who was not incontinent, found the assaults on him utterly degrading. After two nights of continually disturbed sleep Mr Sykes felt demoralized, demotivated and in no hurry to go to work.

At 05.04 a.m. on 31st October 2018, Mr Sykes was abruptly woken. He went to the bathroom. He heard then saw a television was on in another room. Mr Sykes had turned it off the previous evening; he knew it was a favourite trick of Mr. Klemp to turn on the television, even to watch it. Mr Sykes went in the bathroom. Suddenly he was hit from behind at the bladder area. He urinated involuntarily into his pants, enough to soil them. Mr Sykes completed his business then returned to the bedroom. The bed appeared covered by dark entities. Mr Sykes removed several; they were thought creations and can be 'picked up' by thought. He got on the bed. A creature like a large bat, with wings spread out, was fixed to his back. Mr Sykes was hit by power in the back right shoulder. He was unable to sleep. He recorded the incident. It was then 5.33 a.m.

On 1st November 2018 Mr. Klemp appeared to Mr Sykes by projection from the US (where he habitually resides) and said: 'You will never have a trial. You will be terminated.' He looked grim and serious. I treat that accordingly. He is a criminal who belongs in prison.

Note: this is not Mr. Klemp's first death threat. He has form in this area. He previously told Mr Sykes he would make him ill (now done), would 'make you an old man', and on approximately six occasions during 2018 promised he would kill Mr Sykes. On these occasions he made statements including:

'You will never get into the court room;'

'I will make you an old man;'

'You will not make it to the court;'

'You will not be allowed to live.'

This is typical of the cult's threats. They recall the threats of Twitchell's books noted above (at paragraph 11). In approximately March – April 1993 Ebenezer Egunjobi ('Ben'), a Nigerian member of the group in Britain, gave Mr Sykes, who was considering resigning from the cult: 'You will suffer a quick death.' While typical of the thuggish style of that person, it reflects the cult's attitude to noncompliance.
On 6th November 2018, while Mr Sykes had breakfast, Mr. Klemp appeared, glaring with hatred at Mr Sykes, then at the breakfast. The coffee changed taste. The cup was full of slimy water. When Mr Sykes got dressed, Mr. Klemp placed filthy hoods on him repeatedly. Violent entities appeared in front of Mr Sykes, on his jumper, as he put it on.

On 3rd December 2018 Mr Sykes recorded the following pattern of attacks from Mr. Klemp:

(1) appearing in his home, sitting on his chairs, hanging in the air over the bed,

(2) projecting demonic-type creatures onto his head when back at home, otherwise in public places,

(3) subjecting him to intense pressure on the bladder and lower intestine/anal passage to visit the toilet in public places (Mr Sykes is not incontinent, but it is noted Mr. Klemp is obsessed with his private parts (principally his penis and anus),

(4) imposing 'hoods' on his head causing temporary disorientation until Mr Sykes was forced to stop work and remove them,

(5) presenting knives swords and sharp sticks in front of Mr Sykes, then shoving them into his stomach or in the back of his head,

(6) ordering Mr Sykes to return to the Eckankar group, by reason of his responsibility for the torture and killing of vast numbers of people in the distant past, when Mr. Klemp insists Mr Sykes was historic or mythical people such as Genghis Khan, Henry VIII, Shakespeare, Napoleon, and 'Arup' the supposed last ruler of Atlantis.

Bizarre claims of this type are typical of Klemp and Eckankar. Mr. Klemp was apparently using them to induce a feeling of 'guilt' for allegedly causing millions of deaths. Instead of guilt Mr Sykes felt disgust. He regarded Mr. Klemp as a pathetic and vicious criminal. Mr. Klemp abused his telepathic ability to torment Mr Sykes, then tried to confuse his mind with nonsensical claims. Mr Sykes will apply for an order at the appropriate time in the appropriate court that Mr. Klemp is re-detained in a secure psychiatric facility for examination and decision as to his future, as he was in Wisconsin in the early 1970s.

Klemp and Eckankar' violent, vicious harassment in the period preparatory to the commencement of civil proceedings is quite obviously with the intention of dissuading Mr Sykes. Mr Sykes was not, and is not, dissuaded. In essence these are bullying tactics familiar to him from litigation. Quite differently, Mr Sykes seeks orders holding Eckankar and its leader Mr. Klemp to account for their conduct towards him.

On 7th December 2018, when Mr Sykes was on his way to where he was staying, Mr. Klemp projected sensations at Mr Sykes's mind of a reptilian creature landing on his back and clinging on.

He accompanied this freakish routine by abruptly speaking in his normal voice, saying:

'This is really violent isin't it?'

On 11th December 2018 Mr. Klemp followed Mr Sykes home, then as he got off the bus, tried to knock him to the ground. Mr Sykes evaded the attack and kept walking.

On 17th December 2018, as recorded in a prayer request to a Christian church, at 2.40am Mr Sykes went to the bathroom in a hotel bedroom. He felt something approach up behind him. He tried to ignore it. As he walked back to bed, the thing pressed itself upon him. It felt like a reptilian creature or a giant bat, with wings outstretched. Mr Sykes realized it wanted to follow him into the bed. He returned to the bathroom and washed his body where the creature had first pressed on him right hand, right shoulder, top of head. Irritated, Mr Sykes ordered the creature to leave. He saw the semi-transparent form of the creature move away. He returned to the bed and the same happened. He returned to the bathroom, repeated the procedure, and flicked water at it. Now it moved away more definitely. Mr Sykes was able to return to the bed and get on it. with the creature keeping a distance of 3-5 inches. Mr Sykes sat back on the bed, terrified, recovering.

Mr Sykes now realized the real object of Mr. Klemp's attack was to disrupt his sleep. Mr. Klemp attacked him when returning to bed to prevent him going straight back to sleep. Mr. Klemp was determined to prevent deep sleep and rest, and used terror tactics to destroy it.

On 24th December 2018 there was another night attack from Mr. Klemp. When he went to the bathroom he sensed someone, a man, step up fast behind him. This person 'hit' Mr Sykes in the back near the bladder, resulting in instant discharge into his pants. The man glared at Mr Sykes, talking at him. Mr Sykes ignored him. When he returned to the bedroom, he had the impression people were sitting upright on the bed, leaning against the pillows. Mr Sykes chased the entities away. He then got onto the bed, careful to avoid being followed. This time he managed it. He again thought the objective was to wake him completely from his sleepy state until he lost it and any hope of returning to sleep. He heard Mr. Klemp say, 'Well you're awake now.'

On 27th December 2018 Mr Sykes returned from dinner to find the dry sheets he had carefully put on the bed that day were now wet. Mr. Klemp appeared, grinning nastily. Over the holidays Mr Sykes had had suicidal thoughts, finding Mr. Klemp's relentless, determined attack on his sleep patterns intolerable.

Note: making bedsheets wet, or making the bed feel as if it was wet, disturbing Mr Sykes and his sleep was one of Mr. Klemp's favourite forms of assault. Over 26 years he consistently interfered with Mr Sykes's bedsheets by his method of projecting concentrated thought onto them, so as to make them damp, soiled, or filthy.

On 30th December 2018 Mr. Klemp woke Mr Sykes at 3 am. He stood over the bed hitting him until he was awake, disturbed, unable to sleep. Mr Sykes was furious at the violation of his privacy and sleep. Mr. Klemp had destroyed his rest.

8

CONTINUING INCIDENTS OF RITUAL ABUSE

<u>January – February 2019</u>

The following assaults were inflicted on Mr Sykes during January – February 2019.

On 7th January 2019, Mr. Klemp made a new death threat. Communicating by voice only, he appeared to Mr Sykes and said that if he carried on with the case, he would have no choice. Mr Sykes would have to be terminated.

At 1am Mr. Klemp attacked Mr Sykes's holiday hotel bedroom in Thailand. Using concentrated thought projection, Mr. Klemp turned the dry sheets wet, then blasted the bed savagely. Mr Sykes was unable to sleep.

15.3 At 2.30 am, he cut off Mr. Klemp's attack on the hotel bed by stripping and reversing the bed sheets. Only one side had been blasted.

15.4 At 530 am Mr. Klemp hit Mr Sykes in the bathroom after just 3 hours' sleep all night. He placed a stiff, flesh-and-bone cloak on Mr Sykes's back. Mr Sykes went to the bathroom, washed it off, then returned to bed. At which point Mr. Klemp hit him in the back from behind, causing pain in the heart area. That is consistent with his death threat in the day.

15.5 On 10th January 2019 at 7am Mr Sykes went to bathroom after 5 hours' sleep, having worked till after 2am fixing text problems with a document. As he urinated, he felt someone press onto his back. It felt like a male presence, late middle age, 50s-60s. It was likely Mr. Klemp appearing as Paul Twitchell (as he did to cult member Phil Morimitsu as described in his book 'In the company of eck masters'). The male presence followed Mr Sykes back to the bedroom, onto the bed. The man projected something like a thick piece of skin below Mr Sykes's shoulder blades, onto which this male associate directed a maniacal power.

15.5.1 Mr Sykes washed his upper back and arms in the bathroom. He discovered entities on his body. First, there was a large snake's flat head and upper body lying over his head and upper body. This was hard to remove as he could feel the man directing power onto my head to keep the entity there. Mr Sykes removed it by visualisation of a knife that cut into the snakeskin and lifted it off. The attack at once broke off.

Next Mr Sykes removed entities on the back of his neck, including a needle sticking into his neck, onto which violent thought was directed, like sticking an electric needle into his neck. Violent, synthetic little insect-type entities were stabbing and clinging at the same place. These were all created thought entities, but extremely powerful, and if not combated, potentially lethal.

15.5.3   Note: Mr Sykes recorded a note that while during the period 1998 - 2015 he did not record events, trusting Mr. Klemp would eventually stop, when the main part of his adult life had been destroyed, by the age of 60, he decided to sue the cult, which, given his legal training, he knew meant the court would need particulars. He therefore decided to write down Mr. Klemp's assaults in detail.

15.6 On 13th January 2019, on the first night back after the holidays, Mr Sykes's home felt peaceful as he entered. A First Defendant 'thought form' entity tried to follow him in; he threw it off. This type of thought entity was much used by Mr Klemp. Mr Sykes fell asleep watching TV, woke and headed off to bed. As he entered the bedroom Mr Klemp was inside. Mr Klemp sent a violent force at his back. Mr Sykes got on the bed. Mr Klemp projected an image of himself onto Mr Sykes's back and hit him repeatedly. Mr Sykes found it unbearable. He went to the bathroom, washed, moved what appeared to be a snake skin off his head and upper body, and move violent angry maniacal semi-physical entities off him.

15.6.1   Klemp's voice comes clearly into his mind: 'I will let you go to bed.' Mr Sykes got on the bed. He felt very distressed. These words come back to him from 15 years earlier:

'The love of evil,
The cherishing of evil
The worship of evil:
These are the works of Eckankar.'

15.7 On 14th January 2019 at 3.16 am Mr Sykes recorded his prayer request at 3.04 am: 'Please pray to remove the violent cult leader off my back - he is hammering the neck/shoulder blades areas and behind the heart area.' The attack began at about 2.30 am.   It left Mr Sykes completely awake.   He recorded this 'I have to be able to have security in my home and be able to sleep at night.'

15.8 On 16th January 2019 Mr. Klemp's attack was relentless. In the bathroom at about 7am Mr Sykes sensed several creature-like entities, in the shape of tree roots, reaching out to grip his legs, arms and sides. Mr. Klemp was trying to intimidate Mr Sykes out of suing him by attending on him first thing in the morning as well as last thing at night. This was not new: in the past he or various men from the cult Mr Sykes did not recognise, (except one who resembled Paul Twitchell) had visited me to oppress Mr Sykes, apparently to create the idea there was no escaping either the cult-like group or Mr. Klemp. What was new was the insistence of his presence. Mr. Klemp now projected his presence at Mr Sykes daily from his hideaway in Minnesota. Usually this was to ask, with a show of apparent calm, 'What are you going to do?'

15.9 On 17th January 2019 Mr Sykes attended and enjoyed midweek church. He felt Mr. Klemp's presence hanging around, but there was too much love thee (which drives him away) and too much Holy Spirit (which shames him). He attacked early the following morning. Mr Sykes gave up his evening for a client who needed work done urgently. She was pleased and paid for his cab home. He fell on the bed exhausted at 11pm.   At six am he went into the bathroom. It was full of filthy air. He was so sleepy he hardly registered it. Mr Klemp quietly appeared and followed him back into the bedroom. As Mr Sykes walked to the bed, he came up behind him, with an intimidating presence. Then, as Mr Sykes got on the bed, Mr Klemp followed him. He hit Mr Sykes's back with   violent power. Mr Sykes lay unable to sleep, or think, because of the power hitting him. Mr Klemp's voice came through: 'You will not be able to sleep.' That proved true. Finally, Mr Sykes went into the kitchen to take a break. The chairs looked covered with filthy air. Mr Sykes made a snack and sat down to eat it,

His stomach was immediately pushed in by something or someone. He couldn't eat. Mr Sykes then realised someone else was siting there, someone he couldn't see. Mr Sykes felt Mr Klemp's vicious attitude derived from the long series of events between them, dating back to his resignation in 1993, his resignation, his failure to return to the group, for staying a Christian, for suing him in 1998, for preparing to sue him now.

15.10   On 19th January 2019, Saturday night, Mr Sykes went home. The next morning he intended to attend church. Before he got there, Mr Klemp's presence was close, almost suffocatingly. Mr Sykes wondered why. He heard Mr Klemp's voice, as if from a distance: 'Because of church.'

15.11On Sunday 20th January 2019 at 6 am, in the bathroom Mr Sykes felt a creature or a cloak come onto his left side, from the middle up to the shoulder, and attach itself. Mr Sykes tried shooing it away. It didn't move. Then another creature came up and attached itself on his right side, from the middle up to right shoulder. Mr Sykes decided to ignore them and returned to bed. He couldn't sleep. The right side creature hit him remorselessly. The left side creature stabbed him under the left shoulder blade, in the back, directly opposite his heart. Pain shot through him from this stabbing. Through all this he felt Klemp's satisfaction. He had successfully destroyed Mr Sykes's sleep.

15.11On 21st January 2019 Mr Sykes was reading in bed when he looked up and saw Mr. Klemp above him, staring down at him. Like a bat or the older Batman in Batman v Superman, Mr. Klemp's eyes were full of hate. He directed a smashing power onto Mr Sykes's back. Followed by a thin projection of a powerful thought in the form of a cloak, onto which he hit Mr Sykes relentlessly. Mr Sykes was close to screaming. Mr Sykes began to panic, thinking he would again be denied sleep. He was already very tired because of Mr. Klemp's sleep deprivation techniques. Mr. Klemp said in a clear soft voice:

'No-one can take this. No one can do without sleep.'

Mr. Klemp was giving Mr Sykes a clear choice: drop his lawsuit or go without sleep.

15.12   At 4.37am, returning from the bathroom, as Mr Sykes lay down on the bed he felt he was lying on a person. Who was invisible and filthy. He heard Mr. Klemp say, 'Most people would find this terrifying.'

15.13   At 7.10 am Mr. Klemp waited behind Mr Sykes until he had almost finished urinating in the bathroom, then hit him with violent thought power in the lower back, pushing hard on the bladder. Urine splattered out uncontrollably onto the floor, into his pants. Mr Klemp relaxed, enjoying the scene as Mr Sykes cleaned the floor and himself.

15.14   On 22nd January 2019 Mr Sykes recorded that in the week commencing 15th January 2019 Mr. Klemp sent thought impressions at him, threatening three times that he would die if he issued proceedings. To Mr Sykes, a legal practitioner, leaving aside the unusual communication method, these were homicide threats. Mr. Klemp had a documented history of psychiatric detention. What was unclear was how he planned to murder Mr Sykes. Presumably he planned to use either local agents, or perhaps contractors hired in Chicago or Los Angeles

15.15   On 23rd January 2019, at approximately 7pm, Mr. Klemp appeared as a faint presence nearby Mr Sykes's desk and informed him he had to go out to eat. Mr Sykes ignored him. Mr. Klemp´s affected 'concern' for his welfare, after 26 years of violent thought control, left Mr Sykes cold. Abruptly Mr. Klemp flashed an image of Mr Sykes´s bedroom into his mind.   Mr. Klemp´s attitude shifted to nasty. It seemed a threat. Later that night, at about 11pm, when Mr Sykes was watching 'The Big Lebowski' on Netflix, Mr. Klemp's presence returned. Mr. Klemp said: ´It´s time to go to bed. If you can get on the bed.' When the film finished at about 1am, Mr Sykes got ready for bed in the bedroom. Mr. Klemp´s voice was audible, saying, 'Stop. Give it up.' Mr Sykes went to the bathroom, returned, and sensed an entity waiting for him, the length of the window wall. Mr Sykes got into bed. He felt the entity follow him, close around his back. Mr Sykes felt power hitting his back remorselessly. He sensed Mr. Klemp watching, apparently pleased. It was impossible to sleep. Mr Sykes returned to the bathroom, washed his back neck and head, releasing the entity off him. Mr. Klemp appeared, trying to attach new entities. Mr Sykes fended him off. Mr Sykes recorded the event at 5.12 am. He had not slept.

15.16   On Saturday 26th January 2019, at about 11am, while on a train, Mr Sykes heard Mr. Klemp's voice nearby: 'I am going to destroy your weekend.' Mr Sykes felt a thin sharp blade cut into his stomach. It was extremely painful. He realised technically Mr. Klemp was projecting the thought of a sharp knife cutting into him, but that did not reduce the pain. Mr. Klemp had long had the skill to cause pain remotely using concentrated thought. He took control of his target´s mental processes and caused him or her to believe the pain. Following the knife attack, there was constant pressure hitting Mr Sykes´s stomach. Mr Sykes changed trains. He sat in a particular seat. As he did so, Mr. Klemp hit the filthy air behind him with raw violent power. Mr Sykes felt he was being fried, like onions bits in a saucepan

15.17   On 29th January 2019 at 1.22am Mr Sykes sent his church a prayer request asking for relief from Mr. Klemp's attack. That consisted of hitting Mr Sykes with a violent concentrated power on his back, neck and the back of his head. Mr Sykes found it unbearable and extremely distressing. His prayer request said:

'Please pray to remove the psychotic cult leader from my rental bedroom in France. He hit me so hard getting on the bed, directing a smashing power at my back neck and back of head, I could not stand it. Finally I broke the power by washing those parts with cold water, removing a bunch of entities clinging there. This lunatic is still in the bedroom, or projecting his horrid personality at me.'

15.18　　On 3rd February 2019 Mr Sykes coughed up bloody phlegm. Mr. Klemp appeared, watching, and said, 'Cancer. I warned you, if you did not stop.' Previously he said he was holding Mr Sykes´s ´karma´ in the form of intestinal cancer, inherited from his 'incarnation' as Napoleon. Mr Sykes´s mother had died of it, like Napoleon's mother. Mr. Klemp said if Mr Sykes actually attacked the cult, he would stop it, and Mr Sykes would die.

15.19　　On 4th February 2019 Mr Sykes went to fill the kettle in the kitchen. Mr. Klemp's presence appeared behind him. As he poured the water in, it appeared filled with slime. Mr Sykes rebuked Mr. Klemp, who backed off. Mr Sykes made coffee, and filled a glass with water for a vitamin C drinks. Both tasted slimy.

15.20　　On 5th February 2019 Mr Sykes felt war-weary. He recorded: "'Day after day goes by. Mr. Klemp is relentless in attacking me.' He filled a glass with water over a vitamin C capsule. It tasted of slime.

15.21　　Later in the day Mr. Klemp appeared to Mr Sykes and asked, in a cold tone, 'Are you going to church tomorrow?' Two weeks previously Mr Sykes went to a Sunday service, enjoying it. For the next three days Mr Klemp hit him through the day and at night with stunning violence. He didn't go last Sunday. The clear implication of Mr Klemp's question was, if he dared attend, he was going to hit him again.

15.22   On 17th February 2019, Mr Sykes recorded that in the last few weeks Mr. Klemp had appeared to him stating: 'We're going to have to kill you.' That morning Mr. Klemp Klemp stopped him going to church on Sunday morning (something Mr Sykes loved).
He used a familiar tactic: repeatedly disrupting Mr Sykes's sleep, waking him up every 45-60 minutes, pressurising his bladder to force a bathroom trip. Left alone, Mr Sykes did not go to the bathroom with that frequency. Result: by morning he was exhausted. He was desperate to sleep. At that point Mr Klemp left. Mr Sykes slept, and woke up too late to attend church.

15.23   On 24th February 2019 Mr Sykes was too tired to attend church. He did not feel able to take the violence from the cult that comes after church. At night, Mr. Klemp woke Mr Sykes every hour, pressurizing him on the abdomen, by the bladder. In exhaustion Mr Sykes wondered aloud, 'Why are they doing this?' Immediately Mr. Klemp said: 'Because I don't want you to sleep.'

March 2019

16.   The following assaults were inflicted on Mr Sykes during March 2019.

16.1 On 11th March 2019 at 6.33 am, as Mr Sykes left the bedroom to go to the bathroom, he saw a creature like a stick insect but the size of a small man get off the floor and get onto the bed. Mr Sykes ignored it. When he got back into bed, between the sheets there was a yellowish, thick air. Suddenly he was stabbed mid-back by what felt like an insect sting, only large size. He turned around to the wall behind the bed and saw a black creature on the wall. Mr Sykes told it to leave and it left. The foul air remained.

16.2 On Sunday 10th March 2019, at 4.05am. it was freezing. Once again Mr. Klemp was keeping Mr Sykes awake to ensure he was too exhausted by lack of sleep to attend Sunday morning church. When he came back from the bathroom half an hour earlier, Mr. Klemp put an animal cloak hard on his back. Mr Sykes removed it and returned to bed. Mr. Klemp followed him, and slid the animal cloak down his back. Mr Sykes found this revolting. He got out of bed and headed to the bathroom. He heard Mr. Klemp's voice call after him: 'You'll never get it off.' Mr Sykes removed the animal cloak, but back in the bedroom new animal skins were placed on his back.

16.3 On 11th March 2019 Mr Sykes returned home tired, having had no dinner, and went into the sit in the kitchen to make a sandwich. He was hit from behind, both sides, and stabbed hard in the stomach. He opened the window, bring in cold but fresh air. The attack instantly faded.

16.3.1 At this point in time Mr. Klemp´s projections were of two types:

(1) pure thought, entering the mind, creating disturbing sensations, or sheer violent power hitting the senses; or

(2) quasi-physical thought entities, always violent and often terrifying, including the animal cloaks, thick hoods, creatures strapped on Mr Sykes's sides and back, among others.

16.3.2 Mr. Klemp has had form for 45 years as an adult practitioner of thought-based powers. In his autobiography he records how, sitting at his factory desk, he introduced a stream of power into the workplace so violent and powerful everyone around him was disturbed.

16.4 On 12th March 2019, by 5.39 am, Mr. Klemp had kept Mr Sykes awake most of the night. Mr Sykes went to bed on clean sheets. Mr. Klemp appeared and projected a wide, thick, rough animal skin onto his back that felt like dried flesh.

16.5 On 16th March 2019 Mr. Klemp attacked Mr Sykes in the gym (as he had in 1992). He hit Mr Sykes repeatedly in the face and the back of the head while he was swimming. Mr Sykes could not see him but felt his presence. The result was it was hard to swim. The exercise was distracted and spoilt.

16.6 On 23rd March 2019 Mr Sykes woke on Monday morning exhausted by sleep deprivation. What feel like iron bars stabbed into the back of his head, with filthy cloaks and hoods put on his back and head, with Mr Klemp's voice telling him not to pursue the law case, had prevented sleep. He was, again, too tired to make church. Klemp had restored his routine of interfering with Mr Sykes's sleep on Friday, Saturday and Sunday nights. His plan appeared to be to revert to making every single weekend of Mr Sykes's life wretched through broken sleep. The calculation was he would be too tired to attend Sunday church.   Mr Sykes had resorted to finding churches to attend during the week, but he kept up his hateful system.

16.7 On 25th March 2019, Monday, as Mr Sykes finished work at about 10 pm Mr Klemp appeared, watching. He looked crazy. It was like a scene from Morimitsu's 'In the company of Eck Masters', except Mr Klemp's intent was nasty, personal and destructive. Mr Sykes then remembered that Mr Klemp had appeared earlier in the day, twice, and said, 'Tomorrow's Tuesday.' This was another reference to his attacking Mr Sykes Friday-Tuesday every weekend from 1994, because the latter became a Christian who went to church on Sunday. Mr Sykes guessed this meant Mr Klemp intended to attack him. When Mr Sykes left work, Mr Klemp followed him out of the building, up the road, onto a bus. Mr Sykes realised he wanted to attack, and felt he should relax. He stopped off at a bar for a late drink. He did some work on his laptop and felt better. He went home, watching TV while Mr Klemp watched him. Abruptly Mr Klemp shoved him in the stomach a few times. Mr Sykes then went to bed and slept till 4.20am. He went to the bathroom. Mr. Klemp stood behind him, talking at his back. Mr Sykes ignored him and went back to the bedroom. Mr Klemp followed him onto the bed (no one should ever have to experience this, it is so creepily weird). As Mr Sykes got on the bed, Mr Klemp slipped a layer of filthy air onto the sheets underneath him. Mr Sykes experienced being hit from behind while he was, watching. Mr Sykes went to the bathroom. As he opened the door, the bathroom looked filthy. Mr Klemp said, 'Welcome to hell.' Mr Sykes washed and sensed a long snake attached to the top and back of his head. Using focused thought, learned from Mr Klemp by observation and experience over this prolonged period, Mr Sykes lifted the snake or thought form off him. He went back to the bedroom. He did not sleep. At 4.42 am Mr Sykes recorded he was 'sleep-deprived, and not ok.'

16.8 On 26th March 2019, at 5.38 am, Mr Sykes finally gave up trying to sleep. Mr Klemp hovered by the bed. There were at least five other people hovering faintly around the bed. Mr Sykes was being hit by power directed into the sheets under his body. He looked at the sheets. They were covered with 'created thought' blankets, like multiple layers of thin white pastry lying on top of each other. Mr Klemp was projecting a smashing power onto these layers. Finally, Mr Sykes got up, shooed the watchers out of the room, which made it feel lighter and cleaner. Mr Sykes went into the kitchen and recorded the incidents. Mr Klemp watched Mr Sykes type this from behind.

16.9 On 27th March 2019 Mr. Klemp remorselessly deprived Mr Sykes of sleep. He usually woke Mr Sykes at precisely 3 – 5 hours. That night he cut it at 5 hours. At 7am Mr Sykes awoke with pressure on his bladder. He went sleepily to the bathroom, intending only to return to bed and sleep. When he re-approached the bed, Mr. Klemp hit him from behind, and fixed a kind of animal skin to his right shoulder. Mr Sykes got on the bed. The sheets were covered with filthy air, and what felt like entities placed on them. Mr. Klemp stood over him and hit his back and right shoulder with power. With distress and frustration, Mr Sykes got up, went back to the bathroom to wash, and found half a giant snakeskin lying on his head and behind it. It was firmly fixed on his head. He tried to return to bed. Mr. Klemp's attack got worse. Mr Sykes gave up trying to sleep and watched an old film, taking a snack and drinking milk. Mr. Klemp stood watching. After 20 minutes his attack fell off. The film, milk, and oat biscuits worked. Mr Sykes realised Mr. Klemp had established violent entities around the back of his head, which had been hitting me in the back of the head. Mr Sykes washed again, and removed three snakeskins off the top of his head. He returned to bed. A rush of violent power joined and accompanied him as he reached the bed. It was now 8.30 am.

THE SECRET WAY: RITUAL ABUSE IN ECKANKAR

9

MORE INCIDENTS OF RITUAL ABUSE

<u>April – August 2019</u>

17.   The following assaults were inflicted on Mr Sykes during April – August 2019.

17.1 On 8th April 2019 Mr. Klemp appeared to Mr Sykes as a practically physical presence, that he could almost feel and see. He said in a gentle voice, `Don't do it.` Mr Sykes ignored him. Mr. Klemp repeated, `Don't do it.' Mr Sykes ignored him. Mr. Klemp looked into the Plaintff`s face and said, 'We will not be able to let you live.'

17.2 On 3rd May 2019 Mr. Klemp appeared in front of Mr Sykes and appeared to stick pieces of hard grey material into the area immediately in front of his heart. Mr Sykes felt pressure there. He discovered Mr Klemp had already put a string of them onto him in the same place, pressing in on him. It was a clear death threat.

17.3 Mr Sykes recalled that approximately a week before, about the 26th April 2019, Mr Klemp made his first attempt at his new trick. He appeared close in front of Mr Sykes and moved towards him. His hand came out holding a dark grey hard piece of material which he pressed onto Mr Sykes's upper left quadrant, over his heart. It hurt. The piece looked like a fragment of stone tile, that you might pave a patio with. Mr Sykes quickly used directed thought to remove the piece. The pain stopped. It had been a murder threat. Then Mr Klemp said clearly, 'I can kill you now, any time if I want to.'

17.4 On 4th May 2019 Mr. Klemp woke Mr Sykes after 3 ½ hours´ sleep (yet again). Mr Sykes felt there was a creature attached hard to his upper back and head. Mr. Klemp stuck what appeared to be pieces of hard grey material into the skin in front of the heart. Mr Sykes felt unwelcome pressure in his heart area. Mr Sykes next discovered Mr. Klemp had already put a string of hard grey needles onto Mr Sykes in the same place, pressing in on him. Mr Sykes treated this as a clear death threat. He heard Mr. Klemp say clearly, 'I can kill you now, any time if I want to.'

17.5 On 6th May 2019 Mr. Klemp made another death threat. Mr Sykes was getting dressed. Mr. Klemp appeared, seemingly energised, walking around the bedroom, talking. He said, 'If you don't stop, we're not going to bother any longer with these methods. [ie, his torture methods]. We're going to terminate you.'

17.6 On 7th May 2019, Sunday, following a pleasant trip to a foreign church on Sunday, the backlash. Sunday night, returning to his hotel, Mr Sykes found the faint presences of men sleeping in his bed, three next to each other, and tall male forms hanging around the bed on the window side. Mr Sykes rebuked them and commanded them to leave, which they did. He then methodically removed wet layers of air imposed on the bottom sheet. Finally, he slept. Mr Klemp woke him every hour of the night with bladder pressure.

17.7 The following night, 8th May 2019, was unexpectedly violent. The bed had been changed. The clean peaceful sheets brought a furious reaction. Mr Klemp appeared and hung around while I worked on the table ignoring it all. As soon as the cleaner left, and Mr Sykes went in to the bedroom to take off his jacket, Mr Klemp followed him and threw filthy cloaks on the pillow area of the bed. Mr Sykes checked and found the clean sheets were covered with filthy layers by the head. The bottom end of the sheets were clean. He moved the sheets around. When a few minutes later he got on the bed, he was hit from behind. Mr Klemp was in the room, projecting creatures at Mr Sykes's head and back. Next Mr Klemp attached himself to Mr Sykes, who fought with him for some time to get him off me. Finally he slept. After three hours, in a bathroom trip, Mr Sykes found there was a large living entity on his back, pressing on him; it was about 1½ feet thick near his upper back. Mr Sykes felt in a very bad way. His body wanted sleep. He was not able to sleep again.

17.8 On 8th May 2019 at 00.52 am, Mr Sykes emailed a prayer request which stated: 'Please pray to drive the evil spirits off me and the sheets and out of the bedroom. I am exhausted by nightly disturbed sleep and sleep-deprivation. I looked in the mirror and saw my clean features changed deliberately. Eye shadow, then red lines underneath, one, then two, now three. All in the last two months. I am being deliberately exhausted and made old!!'

17.9 On 9th May 2019 at 5.24 am Mr Sykes emailed for prayer, asking: 'Please pray for spiritual cleansing of the bed area and around me, of the cult leader and his octopus-like entities he has put around me and the damp in the sheets. The octopi are horror movie stuff. The damp filthy surfaces on the sheets are disgusting. I keep removing all this stuff and he keeps putting it back!'

17.10	On 13th May 2019 at 21.43 pm, Mr Sykes emailed for prayer, stating: 'Klemp followed me in the office today and hit every part by directing violent blasts of power at it. His mood was angry, grim, determined. I tried sitting on my office chair three times. I couldn't stay more than a few minutes. The third time he stood over me and hit me with a
crazed black power. I could not stand it. He said in a clear voice: 'You have a choice.' I took that to mean: obey me, stop your law case, or suffer.'

17.11Mr Sykes recalled that for the previous two weeks Mr Klemp had hit him daily and nightly. He had had diarrhoea every day, slightly controlled by medication. Mr Klemp kept presenting a belt of black needles to him, then pressing it into his stomach. At night he woke Mr Sykes every 45-60 minutes. Mr Sykes realised that when he slept, Mr Klemp drained him of energy. When he was with people with whom there was a love relationship, Mr Klemp could not come in. Love bars his way. He has to wait until Mr Sykes is alone, then applies his needles or entities to drain up to what felt like 60% of Mr Sykes's body energies, leaving him feeling weak, without energy or drive, uninterested in activity.   When people pray for Mr Sykes, Mr Klemp leaves. He cannot stay in the presence of holiness. But Mr Klemp's attack overall has been frequent enough to have wrecked Mr Sykes's general state of health. His attack on sleep and digestion has been unremitting.

17.12	On 14th May 2019, at 04.01 am, Monday, Mr Sykes emailed for prayer, asking: 'Please pray to remove the violent cult leader Klemp from my bedroom. He has been hitting me and the bedsheets with psychotic violent power. Just horrible. He has come I think to punish me for attending church yesterday morning and taking someone with me!'

17.13   On 18th May 2019, Saturday morning, when Mr Sykes was desperate to catch up sleep, Mr Klemp pressured his bladder forcing him to go to the bathroom.   Mr Klemp appeared to him in the bathroom and stuck daggers in his stomach.

17.14   On 23rd May 2019 at 05.26 am, after Mr. Klemp had repeatedly attacked Mr Sykes at night in his bedroom on 23rd, 28th and 29th May 2019, he woke Mr Sykes after three hours' sleep to the minute. Mr Sykes washed a 'skin' off his head and back. Back in the bedroom, he still could not sleep. He heard Mr. Klemp say, 'And I will not stop.'

17.15   On 24th May 2019, Thursday, at 5.17 am Mr Sykes recorded that Mr Klemp had kept him awake all night.   Mr Sykes was too tired and distracted to go to church. Mr Klemp delayed him until he was broken and unable to do anything until he had recovered.   Mr Klemp put tormenting, moving thought control-created entities on Mr Sykes's neck and head as I put on a business shirt, then fed the entities into the shirt, the sleeves, onto his face, until it was unbearable to Mr Sykes. He went to a cafe, hardly able to walk. He drank over a litre of water and two coffees before he began to feel grounded. After an hour he was okay to travel. He arrived near the church exactly at the time the service ended. That night Mr Sykes determined to attend another service. Mr Klemp appeared and said, 'Don't go home. Stay at a hotel.' Mr Sykes set off home. Mr Klemp followed him, and said, 'You don't want to go home.' Mr Sykes went home. He got comfortable on the bed and for two seconds had peace. As he turned off the light, something alive seemed to come onto my back, underneath him, onto the sheets, onto the back of his head. Mr Klemp's maniacal presence was intense in the room.   He hit Mr Sykes continuously until he gave up and went to record the incident.

17.16   On 30th May 2019 Mr Klemp attacked his intestine from stomach down to anus. It was yet another day of semi-diarrhoea. Mr Sykes heard Klemp say: 'You will be an invalid.'

17.17   On 31st May 2019 at 03.02 am, Mr Sykes emailed for prayer complaining of torment by a man leering at him, glaring at him from behind, and projecting a strange yellow light at Mr Sykes through his skin.

17.18   On 3rd June 2019, at 01.07 am, Monday, Mr Sykes noted Mr Klemp and a number of indistinct persons who appeared to be in agreement with him, and therefore probably members projecting from the USA, were running an all night attack. Mr Sykes was in a hotel. The men were standing around the bed, like shadows. Hour after hour, Mr Klemp hit Mr Sykes on his body, particularly on the back of his neck. The men hit Mr Sykes with power, and tried to fix animal skins on his back.

17.19   On 8th June 2019 at 03.01 am, Mr Sykes recorded he lay down to sleep after a long tiring day at work, but did not sleep. He was hit continually from behind. There was an animal skin cloak placed on his back and head. Mr Sykes had removed one like it in the bathroom earlier. Another now lay under him. It was impossible to sleep.

17.20   On 10th June 2019 at 6.35 am, Mr Sykes emailed for prayer stating Mr Klemp had appeared at 6 am, an hour before the alarm set for 7 am, and had stood at the end of the bed and directed showers of filth onto the sheets. Mr Sykes felt something hard slip under his right shoulder. He could not sleep. He got off the bed to remove the filth off the sheets with concentrated thought. Mr Klemp simply directed more layers onto the bed. All the prayer, peace and cleanliness disappeared. 'I've done it,' Mr Sykes heard Mr Klemp say. Mr Sykes started to write the email. He felt the sheets burn underneath him, apparently to distract him.

17.21   On 11th June 2019, Mr Klemp appeared to Mr Sykes on the way home. He said, 'You don't want to know what is in store for you at home.' When Mr Sykes sat in his kitchen to eat toast and watch TV to relax, Mr Klemp hit him in the stomach. When he went to the bedroom, Klemp fixed a creature onto his back neck and head. It was under Mr Sykes as he lay down. He got off the bed and shrugged off the entity. It was put straight back on him. Mr Sykes then suffered a gruelling night of attack from Mr Klemp, who woke him every 45 minutes through pressure on his bladder. When Mr Sykes got up, he was exhausted by lack of sleep. His eyes burned with lack of rest.

17.22   On 12th June 2019, Saturday night, Mr Klemp presented a creature to Mr Sykes as he got on the bed, that was abruptly fixed on Mr Sykes's head and which stabbed his back, neck and head. Mr Sykes became concerned that if he carried out his plan to attend church the following morning, Sunday, he would suffer violent reprisals from Mr Klemp. Mr Sykes could not bear another smash attack.

17.23   On 15th June 2019, at 07.03 am, Mr Sykes emailed for prayer, recording that every time he fell asleep, Mr Klemp woke him up, hitting his body. Mr Klemp had fixed creatures onto his shoulder blades, upper back and head. Through fatigue Mr Sykes could no longer cope.

17.24   In or about the first two weeks of June 2019, as recorded on 8th and 16th June 2019, Mr Klemp presented another of his 'belts' to Mr Sykes. Mr Klemp appeared standing directly in front of him. Mr Sykes found his gaze focussed onto Mr Klemp's hands, held in front of him. In Mr Klemp's hands was a belt about two inches high, thick, with the appearance of an old-fashioned leather belt. The front faced Mr Sykes. It was studded with tiny black needles. Mr Klemp pressed the belt into Mr Sykes's stomach. He felt instantly unwell.

17.24.1   At this point Mr Sykes examined his stomach. He lifted off several black, shapeless entities and saw underneath hundreds of tiny needles. Mr Sykes realised Mr Klemp had been causing him diarrhoea by the application of these needle-packed entities. Mr Sykes guessed Mr Klemp did so at night when Mr Sykes slept. Mr Sykes assumed the needles irritated the intestines, causing an inflammation that prevented his digestion working properly, and causing the content to be shovelled down the intestines in a rapid, water-sodden expulsion.

17.24.2   For the avoidance of doubt, Mr Sykes avoided foods that could irritate his intestines. Secondly, he did not seek medical or hospital examination as he found over-the-counter medication controlled the condition. He used the medication only for a day, to avoid dependence. The condition did not disappear. Mr Sykes sensed Mr Klemp could make him much more ill with a more forceful application of the same methods, to the point of terminating his life. Mr Sykes considers Mr Klemp did not do so, as his purpose was not primarily to cause Mr Sykes injury, but to give him an objective choice of obey or suffer. His ultimate purpose was to cause Mr Sykes to give up the fight and submit to his will.

17.24.3   However, the emotional/physical effect of these attacks was to cause Mr Sykes daily diarrhoea and accompanying physical weakness.

17.25   On or about 15th June 2019 Mr Klemp appeared to Mr Sykes and stabbed him with a black sword. It was not straight, but angled halfway up at 35 degrees. It was jagged, and uneven in width. It was not like a human sword from the past. It was different, looked powerful and was full of a controlled, contained violence. Mr Klemp stuck the sword straight into Mr Sykes's stomach. Mr Sykes fought him off, pushing him away, using his own power of thought to push away Mr Klemp's projected presence. Once done, Mr Sykes put his hand on the sword and removed it. For the avoidance of doubt, this was not a physical sword, and Mr Sykes did not remove it with a physical hand. The sword was a complex thought, given shape and form by Mr Klemp, and empowered with his own emotions. Mr Sykes removed it by his own power of thought.

17.25.1   During 26 years of violent attack by Mr Klemp, Mr Sykes developed to a modest degree, and depending on his sleep level and state of health, the ability to fight thought with thought.   Further, for the avoidance of doubt, Mr Klemp was at all material times a highly trained and expert practitioner of telepathy (the ability to project thought into the mind of a third party over whom he has or can establish influence) and thought control (the ability to control remotely the thought content of the mind of the third party over whom he has or can establish influence).   In addition to controlling the thought content of the third party's mind, Mr Klemp was able to control the content of the third party's senses (feeling, seeing, hearing, touching, etc). Subject to the volitional agreement of the third party, Mr Klemp could at all material times control the immediate material environment of the third party.

17.25.2   Mr Klemp came back fast with two more stabbing swords. Mr Sykes was stabbed, but was able to remove them.

17.26   On approximately 26th June 2019 Mr. Klemp appeared close in front of Mr Sykes and moved towards him. His put a dark grey hard piece of material, like a fragment of stone onto Mr Sykes` chest in front of his heart.   The immediate effect was pain in that area.
Mr Sykes moved quickly and, using the same technique of directed thought, removed the piece. The pain stopped. It was another threat to kill. Mr Sykes recalled the previous night he

heard Mr. Klemp say clearly, 'I can kill you now, any time if I want to.'

17.27 On 19th June 2019, at 5.30 am, Mr Klemp woke Mr Sykes out of sleep after 2.5 hours' sleep, Mr Sykes having worked late. Mr Sykes woke with a clear mental image that his bowels had loosened into his underwear. He went to the bathroom as fast as he could. When he got there, he realised it was an illusion. Klemp stood there watching him, a malicious expression on his face. Mr Sykes returned to the bedroom. As he got on the bed, Mr Klemp placed a large 'skin', a kind of animal skin interior, around him. Mr Sykes lay on the bed. The skin made his flesh creep, but he ignored it, on the principle that if he resisted, Mr Klemp would attack harder. Mr Klemp directed a continuous blast of power or focussed energy onto the exterior of this skin, sufficient to disturb Mr Sykes and prevent him falling asleep. This was the second night of reduced sleep, Mr Klemp having woken him the previous night after 3 hours then kept him awake.

17.28 On 22nd June 2019, Saturday, at 3.41 am, Mr Sykes emailed for prayer in these terms:

'Please pray to remove the violent, psychotic cult leader Harold Klemp from my bedroom. It's my first night back after a week away, and he is desperate to attack. He knows this place, so he hones right onto it as soon as he senses I'm back. He has already hit me for two hours continually in the kitchen, while I was eating my tiny dinner, by hitting me from behind, then ordering me repeatedly to obey him and go to bed. As soon as I went into the bedroom, I saw the change: cloaks of filthy air draped over the bed, like a spider would. I am dead tired and need rest and his obsessive presence gone.'

17.29 In the week commencing 17th June 2019, Mr Klemp imposed a harder regime of sleep deprivation and intestinal attack. On Tuesday 18th, and Wednesday 19th, he woke the

Plaintiff after 3 hours' sleep. He imposed semi-diarrhoea Mr Sykes every day. Mr Sykes considered he was being left just enough sleep and nutrition to stay alive.

17.30   On 23rd June 2019 Mr Sykes stayed in a hotel near the office to have an early start. Mr Sykes needed to do a great deal of office work. Mr. Klemp would not be able to plan his attack by focusing in advance on Mr Sykes's location, as that would be uncertain until at least room allocation. Mr Sykes had been dodging Mr. Klemp's obsessive focus in ways like this for 26 years. This time Mr. Klemp was ahead of him. He had the ability to discover remotely the room allocation once done. When he walked into the hotel room, it was packed full of black, violent energy. Hanging in the air, mid-level, it was like a storm cloud inside a room. From the edges of the cloud, the room was normal. It was a science fiction movie scene. Mr Sykes ignored it and undressed for bed. Mr. Klemp appeared, crazy with anger. He came up to Mr Sykes, and fixed one octopus-like creature after another to his head. This went on for an hour.

17.31   On 24th June 2019, at about 1 am, Mr Klemp followed Mr Sykes from a hotel bar where he went to relax with a glass of whisky and a newspaper. On the bus home, Mr Klemp attacked. He threw an animal skin under Mr Sykes's rear and up onto his back, then hit the skin with power. Mr Sykes had to fight to control his attention as he was trying to sort out his headphone wires. He got the music going, started reading a book. Mr Klemp stood directly behind him, staring at the book, to interfere with Mr Sykes reading. Mr Sykes persisted and read the book. When Mr Sykes got off the bus he tried again. Mr Klemp pushed the animal skin harder onto his back, extending it over his head and down onto his chest. Mr Sykes found this revolting. Mr Klemp said Mr Sykes was going to be attacked. Mr Sykes ignored him. He went home, turned and told Mr Klemp's slight, ghostly presence he could not enter, and went in. As he walked up a corridor, Mr Sykes felt Mr

Klemp following behind and projecting emotional fear into him. In the kitchen, which was clean and peaceful, Mr Sykes made a sandwich. and sat down to eat it. Mr Klemp hit him from behind, above the left hip. He projected some kind of entity under Mr Sykes's rear. Mr Sykes experienced intense discomfort.

17.32   On 24th June 2019, at 5.23 am, after 3 hours' sleep, Mr Klemp woke Mr Sykes and stood leering over him. Mr Sykes felt his bedsheets burning his back, suffused with a violent power. Mr Sykes pulled on a shirt and lay back. The burning felt less. Without warning an animal skin appeared under his back, through which Mr Klemp hit his upper back with power. He heard Mr Klemp say, 'You will be awake.' Mr Sykes got off the bed to avoid being hit. He looked back at the bed. The sheets appeared covered with layers of black filth and with shapeless entities. To the touch, the upper sheet felt violent. Mr Sykes sensed and half-saw a layer of violent air hanging about 5mm off the surface of the sheet. He heard Mr Klemp say, 'If you commit suicide this stops.'

17.33   On 24th June 2019 Mr Klemp kept Mr Sykes awake until 6.55 am. Mr Sykes finally emailed for prayer. He slept exhausted from 6.55 am to 8.50 am. Mr Sykes had slept exhausted sleep for 3 hours, then 2 hours. In between Mr Klemp had woken him out of deep sleep and made sure he woke fully. This was thorough sleep deprivation. At the same time, Mr Klemp projected thoughts about suicide into his mind. Mr Sykes recorded Mr Klemp's activity as it appeared he was trying to induce Mr Sykes to kill himself to avoid the intended litigation.

17.34   On 25th June 2019 at 8.55 am Mr Sykes advised in an email prayer request that unidentified agents of Mr Klemp had put a creature on his back, and were hitting the creature with power constantly, upsetting Mr Sykes further. He advised Mr Klemp was sending thoughts about suicide, and was trying to obtain his termination of life. Mr Sykes noted if he was a suicidal type, he would have been long gone.

17.35   On 29th June 2019 Mr Klemp appeared to Mr Sykes in a corridor at work. He asked Mr Sykes in a low voice whether he would drop it. Mr Sykes ignored him. Mr Klemp followed him and informed him he was missing out on his spiritual destiny. That was to return to the group. Mr Sykes considered Mr Klemp was still the detainee in the Wisconsin psychiatric facility, dreaming solipsistic dreams unrelated to the reality of the world and the people in it. For the past week or so, every day, without fail, Mr Klemp appeared to Mr Sykes and asked him if he was going ahead with it.

17.36   On 30th June 2019 Mr Sykes went to sit in his office to prepare cross-examination questions for a four day trial commencing 1st July 2019 in a court in Croydon Employment Tribunal. Mr Sykes had his file, laptop and iced coffee (now hot). As he sat down, the chair was weirdly damp. Violent, electricity-like power smashed into the seat and his rear. He heard Klemp's voice clearly: 'I will get you off this chair.' Mr Klemp appeared and hit him in the back. He projected a shapeless creature made of slimy air and underneath Mr Sykes, who found it revolting. It was another act of ritual abuse, designed to keep Mr Sykes on edge until the next attack. Mr Klemp hit him harder with violent blasts of power, until Mr Sykes could not stand it. He got up. His body felt shot through with violence.

17.36.1   Mr Sykes decided to work on something else, and instead did preparatory work for his personal US case. He went through an early Klemp book and found paragraphs criticising Jesus and putting himself above Him. Mr Sykes posted them online. As he did this the mood in the office changed. The violent atmosphere faded. The room became quiet. He heard a voice say, dolefully, 'We don't want you to do this.'

17.36.2   Two images were presented to Mr Sykes's mind. First, a layer of wet filth was lifted straight off the chair he had first sat on. Second, two wet entities left the bed, whose sheets Mr Sykes had changed earlier.

17.36.3   Mr Sykes put his US case materials away and went back to the trial work. He had recovered from the assault. But two hours had been lost. Mr Sykes, who had to leave at 11 pm, worked till 12, prepping questions for witnesses, and answering client emails.

17.37   On 1st July 2019, at 1 am, Mr Klemp appeared to Mr Sykes in his kitchen. He warned
of the consequences of suing him. Mr Sykes made toast, watched the end of 'The Social Network' on TV, and relaxed. When Mr Sykes went to bed, Mr Klemp came back, in a disturbed mood, projecting unstable violent energies at him. Mr Sykes could not take any more craziness so he emailed for prayer relief. Mr Klemp left. Mr Sykes fell asleep.

17.38   On 1st July 2019, Monday, Mr Klemp appeared to Mr Sykes in a corridor and asked him if he was attending church on Wednesday. On 2nd July 2019 Mr Klemp re-appeared and put the same question. This time his tone was aggressive, menacing. Later, at about 8pm, when Mr Sykes went to eat, he felt needles stabbing into his stomach. On 3rd July 2019, the day for attending church, now practicable as the trial was adjourned on the first day, Mr Sykes suffered uncontrollable liquid diarrhoea. It was unrelated to food intake. Mr Sykes sensed Mr Klemp's contentment

.

17.39   On 2nd July 2019 Mr Klemp appeared to Mr Sykes in the form of the group founder Paul Twitchell. His eyes were burned black. He invited Mr Sykes to return to the cult group.

17.40   On 3rd July 2019, at 4.28am, the night before the midweek church service, Mr Klemp kept Mr Sykes awake to ensure he did not attend the church service. Mr Klemp's mood was crazily violent. Mr Sykes sensed Mr Klemp hated him. This time Mr Klemp directed a laser-like beam into the back of his head, stunning his mind. Mr Klemp threw creatures at him, and covered the bed with violent entities and layers of filthy air. Mr Klemp finally stopped the attack about 7 am. Mr Sykes immediately fell asleep out of sheer fatigue. He woke too late to attend the church service.

17.41   On 4th July 2019 Mr Klemp appeared to Mr Sykes as he opened an envelope containing Cult member Morimitsu's In the Company of Eck Masters and shelved it, ready for use. He sensed Mr Klemp's presence. Mr Klemp was extremely angry. He left and returned after three hours and abruptly hit Mr Sykes's bladder area. Mr Sykes had a sudden uncontrollable desire to go to the bathroom. It was not his desire, which would have gradually increased and be controllable, but sensation imposed on him by Mr Klemp. When Mr Sykes got back from the bathroom, his chair was covered with layers of filth. Mr Klemp hit him with fury from behind, directing blasts of power at his rear, back and onto the seat. This was the real Mr Klemp, his secret violent self, well disguised by his smarmy, smug, noncommittal persona.

17.42   On 8th July 2019 Mr Klemp appeared in Mr Sykes's office, surrounded him with dark, filthy entities, and inserted six inch spikes into the back of his head. Through these spikes he funnelled violence. He was increasing the violence, disturbing me and the environment, displaying the skill he first admitted to in 'Child in the Wilderness' in the print room scene. At 11.11 am Mr Sykes lost his temper with this sustained assault, and shouted at Mr Klemp's shadowy presence, 'What do you want?' Mr Klemp leaned forward towards Mr Sykes and said in a cold, nasty voice: 'You know what you have to do.'

17.43   On 12th July 2019 Mr. Klemp appeared to Mr Sykes and said he was being attacked because of the case he was bringing.

17.44   On 13th July 2019, Saturday, Mr Sykes was eating a good quality steak to gain energy when Mr. Klemp appeared and pointed at his waist. Mr Sykes saw a thick white linen belt around his waist, full of short black needles. The reiterated message was that Mr Klemp could make him ill any time.

17.45   From Saturday 13th to Tuesday 16th July 2019, Mr Klemp projected needles and black implements into Mr Sykes' abdomen.   On Tuesday morning, Mr Sykes had severe diarrhoea. He felt sick and weak all day, and unable to work.

17.46   On 15th July 2019 Mr. Klemp again attacked Mr Sykes at night.   Mr Sykes emailed for prayer at 01.22 am requesting this: 'Please pray to remove the vicious cult leader from this London hotel room (escaping mysterious bed bugs in home).   It was extremely difficult getting on the bed because 5mm behind me, following, was the cult leader. He was hitting the back of my head with power. I got on the bed and found it layered with spider like material, with entities that promptly spewed filthy air onto me. I returned them onto his wife and daughter, naming them. Most of the attack stopped dead. He is still hanging around, malicious and violent.'

17.47   On 19th July 2019 Mr Sykes felt Mr Klemp appear behind him, as he was ordering the US dollar cheque necessary for filing a Complaint in a US District Court. Mr Klemp stood silently behind Mr Sykes in the bank, watching.   When the order was complete, Mr Klemp followed him out of the bank. He was agitated. Mr Sykes felt his agitation growing.

17.48   Mr Klemp's reprisal came when Mr Sykes got home. As he walked to the apartment block, he felt Mr Klemp catch up behind him, then project a badly disturbed presence at him. Mr Klemp was a violent ghost, throwing violent thoughts at him one after another.   As Mr Sykes went inside, Mr Klemp suddenly appeared and attacked Mr Sykes. He was ultra-violent. He hit Mr Sykes repeatedly on the back of the head, shouting at him in a rage, beside himself with anger. Mr Sykes told him he could not enter, pushed back with his own thought Mr Klemp's projections, and went in. Mr Sykes was suddenly aware of a dark, soiling presence following him down the corridor, projecting hate.

17.49   In the kitchen Mr Sykes made a snack while Mr Klemp watched, standing close behind him, radiating anger. Mr Sykes sat down to eat. Mr Klemp interposed himself in front of Mr Sykes and hit him repeatedly with blasts of power in the stomach, on the back, on the sides. Then he said: 'I am going to destroy everything.' He turned and directed violent power into the kitchen, with a crazed violence. Mr Sykes was struck by how extremely violent he was. He pushed Mr Klemp aside, which broke the attack. Mr Klemp stepped back and was silent.

17.50   On 22nd July 2019 in another night attack Mr Klemp hit Mr Sykes's upper back and head continuously for a period of time, then abruptly stabbed him in the lower back with a thin needle.

17.51   On 24th July 2019 at night Mr Klemp appeared behind Mr Sykes in the bedroom. His mood was vicious, disturbed. Mr Sykes got onto the bed. Mr Klemp came up fast behind him and put a creature with five arms on his back. The arms were long and moving about. There was suddenly a burning cloak on his back. Mr Sykes felt he could not stand it. Mr Klemp's satisfied, leering voice said: 'You will have to get up!' Mr Sykes got off the bed to stop the torment. Half an hour later, after many attempts to get on the bed without Mr Klemp's creature following him, Mr Sykes managed to get on the bed while fending off the creature hanging behind him. Mr Klemp hit him on the upper back and back of head continuously. It was clear to Mr Sykes that Mr Klemp was-making sure he could not sleep. Finally, Mr Klemp left when Mr Sykes had to leave. Mr Sykes slept out of exhaustion. He felt he had lived in hell for 26 years since Mr Klemp had begun his attack.

On 29th July 2019 Mr Sykes stayed up till 2.20 during work for Monday (notes from a hearing on Friday and options for the client). He went to bed. He woke 5 hours' later. He felt he had to go to the bathroom. In the bathroom Mr Klemp hit him from behind, and put a wide creature shining with a white-yellow light on his back. Mr Sykes was unable to return to sleep.

The underlying goal of all these night attacks was to remove sleep from his system. There were multiple dividends for Mr Klemp: fatigue later in the day, lack of energy to go to the gym, weight out of control, a weakened and out of condition body.

On 30th July 2019 Mr Klemp appeared in the bathroom when Mr Sykes had slept three hours, and shoved him in the back while urinating. Mr Sykes went back to the bedroom. He was instantly hit by black creatures already on the bed. When Mr Sykes ordered them to leave, they left. He lay down to sleep, on his right. Mr Klemp must have known from long observation Mr Sykes slept on his right. He executed an apparently prepared attack by hitting Mr Sykes viciously on the right shoulder. Next Mr Klemp attached the right side of an animal skin.

On 31st July 2019 Mr Klemp switched back to obstructing Mr Sykes's aim of attending church services. He had briefly flirted with encouraging Mr Sykes to attend, and stopping his campaign of sleep destruction in the 1-3 days before and 1-2 days after the service. Mr Sykes considered that was because he had seen Mr Sykes methodically prepare records of his anti-Christian assaults in advance of pleading them for the court During late June and July 2019 Mr Klemp had appeared before the time Mr Sykes had fixed to attend a particular church, and impudently encouraged him to attend. On 31st July 2019, in his unstable style, flitting in his mind with malicious purpose from one fast point to another, Klemp switched back to attacking church attendance.

Mr Klemp pressured Mr Sykes out of deep sleep into a bathroom visit. He smashed his bladder area with power. When Mr Sykes returned to the bedroom, Mr Klemp stuck a creature on his back. Mr Sykes struggled to get it off him. Finally, he got on the bed, and saw the pillows were covered with creatures. They were laying on layers of filth, as if they were blankets. Mr Sykes was unable to sleep. His night rest was callously disturbed and finally destroyed.

Conclusion

Eckankar's ritual abuse

In the above-cited incidents, which is not a complete record, Klemp and Eckankar inflicted severe and sustained psychological and emotional distress on Mr Sykes.

The said acts had severe and long-term consequences for Mr Sykes's emotional and psychological health7, his bodily health, and his social empathy, leaving him unmarried, without family, with virtually no social life, as he lived a daily battle for 26 years to survive Klemp and Eckankar' assaults on his mind, so as to be able to work and provide for himself.

THE SECRET WAY: RITUAL ABUSE IN ECKANKAR

FURTHER READING

The following books complement
The Secret Way series

Books by J.N.Sykes

The false masters of Eckankar

The sick soul of Paul Twitchell

The Truth about Eckankar

Dark Magic in the Eckankar Cult